La Règle du jeu

V. F. Perkins

palgrave
macmillan

A BFI book published by Palgrave Macmillan

First published in 2012 by
PALGRAVE MACMILLAN

on behalf of the

BRITISH FILM INSTITUTE
21 Stephen Street, London W1T 1LN
www.bfi.org.uk

There's more to discover about film and television through the BFI. Our world-renowned archive, cinemas, festivals, films, publications and learning resources are here to inspire you.

Palgrave Macmillan in the UK is an imprint of Macmillan Publishers Limited, registered in England, company number 785998, of Houndmills, Basingstoke, Hampshire RG21 6XS. Palgrave Macmillan in the US is a division of St Martin's Press LLC, 175 Fifth Avenue, New York, NY 10010. Palgrave Macmillan is the global academic imprint of the above companies and has companies and representatives throughout the world. Palgrave® and Macmillan® are registered trademarks in the United States, the United Kingdom, Europe and other countries.

Front cover design: Andy Bridge
Series text design: ketchup/SE14
Images from *La Règle du jeu*, Nouvelle Édition Française; *La Bête humaine*, Paris Film Production; *La Grande Illusion*, Réalisations d'Art Cinématographique; *Diary of a Chambermaid*, © Camden Productions, Inc.

Set by Cambrian Typesetters, Camberley, Surrey
Printed in China

This book is printed on paper suitable for recycling and made from fully managed and sustained forest sources. Logging, pulping and manufacturing processes are expected to conform to the environmental regulations of the country of origin.

British Library Cataloguing-in-Publication Data
A catalogue record for this book is available from the British Library
A catalog record for this book is available from the Library of Congress
10 9 8 7 6 5 4 3 2 1
21 20 19 18 17 16 15 14 13 12

ISBN 978–0–85170–965–9

Contents

Acknowledgments

This is not an introduction to *La Règle du jeu*, not a book to prepare you for a first viewing of the film. It aims to be helpful once you have seen the movie, preferably more than once. Through decades of fascination with Renoir's work, I have exchanged ideas with, and absorbed insights from, a great parade of friends and colleagues. They may find that I have failed to credit them appropriately for observations that they first brought my way. I know that I owe much to those listed here and I am sure that there are others whom I should have named: Charles Barr, Michael Bell, Stanley Cavell, James Conant, Colin Davis, Christopher Faulkner, Edward Gallafent, Tag Gallagher, Andrew Klevan, Miguel Marias, Valerie Orpen, Gilberto Perez, Alastair Phillips, Douglas Pye, William Rothman, Deborah Thomas, Ginette Vincendeau, George Wilson, Peter Wollen, James Zborowski.

Martin O'Shaughnessy was kindly helpful with my calls on his research. Richard Perkins of Warwick University was, as ever, the most obliging and resourceful librarian one could imagine.

This book is dedicated, in recognition of many critical debts, to the memory of Ian Cameron, Raymond Durgnat and Robin Wood.

1 Making Unmaking Remaking

CAHIERS   To get back to *The Rules of the Game*: Weren't you surprised by the poor reception it got?

RENOIR   Well, I wasn't expecting it. I never expect it, and for a very simple reason: I always imagine that the film I'm going to make will be an extremely marketable film, which will delight all the distributors and will be considered rather ordinary.[1]

Nowadays *La Règle du jeu* starts with an announcement. Before we get to the film itself we are told that we are to see a reconstruction. 'Jean Gaborit and Jacques Durand have reassembled the original version of this film with the approval and guidance of Jean Renoir, who dedicates this resurrection to the memory of André Bazin.' Implied here is a deal of significant context, much of it to do with the startling history of the film's production.

The Gaborit/Durand version is the one presented in triumph at the 1959 Venice Film Festival, twenty years after the calamitous Paris premiere of July 1939. In his memoirs, Renoir looked back from the 1970s on a failure that had so depressed him that he made up his mind either to turn his back on cinema or to leave France. He had been stunned to discover that the film rubbed most of the audience up the wrong way. 'It was a tremendous blow. The film was received with something like hatred … and the public regarded it as a personal insult.'[2]

It was the public, more than the journalistic, response that floored Renoir. He acknowledged that a number of reviewers wrote in praise of the picture. The historian Claude Gauteur assembled a dossier of forty-one contemporary responses and was able to weigh seven completely favourable reviews against twice as many that were unqualified in their hostility.[3] Some revisionist historians wish us to believe that the film's misfortunes were exaggerated, by Renoir among others, to support the legend of the martyred masterpiece. Gauteur, for instance, warns against supposing that the censors made it a special target before and after the outbreak of war. '*La Règle du jeu* was banned from September 1939 to February 1940 on account of the conditions of the time, as were a number of other French films. No more, no less.'[4] Renoir recorded its withdrawal as demoralising.[5] No memorable comfort came from knowing, if he did, that others suffered the same misfortune.

A notion of mastery is proclaimed in much writing about film. It pictures the author of a great work as from the outset certain of the intention, steadfast and confident in its execution. In this respect, forgetfulness worked to foster the image of pure victimhood for Renoir and *La Règle du jeu*. Accounts of the film's reception have tended to overlook the director's own misgivings as it was prepared for release, and to ignore his part in its undoing. It was because of the misgivings, perhaps, that he gave in to the demands of the film's backers. 'Commerce has spoken,' he told his colleagues. 'We are going to make cuts.'[6] As a result, the premiere version of the film had lost 13 minutes from Renoir's first cut; the losses affected a number of scenes and moments that would now be thought indispensable, and they may well have brought additional confusion to what was always an unorthodox storyline.

Panic cutting foresaw, tried to forestall, difficulties at the box office. Anxiety was inevitable when a major triumph was required for the film to realise the hopes, and return the money, invested in it. Since a mere moderate success would be accounted a failure, how terrible it must have been when it was received with worse than indifference. There is little room for doubt that *La Règle du jeu* was widely scorned and hated. Too many people who were there at the time – among others, the actors Marcel Dalio[7] and Paulette Dubost[8], the set designer Eugène Lourié[9] and Henri Cartier-Bresson[10], an assistant director on the film – left testimony that supports Renoir's memory of a painful rejection. In its wake, further cuts were made as the director attempted to get rid of incidents that seemed particularly to rile the spectators, only to find that hostility erupted elsewhere in what remained. The picture shrank from the 113 minutes of its preview version to end up as a range of truncated prints of less than 90. The work of suppression was extended and apparently completed in 1942 by an Allied air raid that demolished the laboratories housing the negative. *La Règle du jeu* had become something beyond a film *maudit*.

If it was France that doomed the film, it was France too that rescued it. After the war, its reputation gathered. More voices joined those that had been raised in 1939 to defend or acclaim it. There came to light an 80-minute version in good condition. At that length, gaps in the continuity must have been evident and tantalising. But the version established itself in the ciné-clubs and specialised houses.

We have two key witnesses to the impact even of the mutilated versions. Alain Resnais, speaking to *Sight & Sound* as the director of *Hiroshima mon amour* (1959) and *La Guerre est finie* (1966), recalled a 1944 screening as the single most overwhelming experience he had ever had in the cinema:

When I came out of the theatre, I remember, I just had to sit down on the edge of the pavement; I sat there for a good five minutes, and then I walked the streets of Paris for a couple of hours. For me, everything had been turned upside down. All my ideas about the cinema had been challenged … Since then, of course, I've seen it at least fifteen times – like most film-makers of my generation.[11]

François Truffaut echoes this theme in a letter to Renoir:

I saw *La Règle du jeu* over and over again between the ages of thirteen and fourteen, when everything in my life was going so badly. [It] helped me to keep going, to understand the motives of the people around me, and to get through those awful years of my adolescence … I will always feel that my life is connected to the film you made.[12]

If we can rely on Truffaut's memory, his immersion in *La Règle du jeu* must have occurred in the immediate aftermath of World War II.

Then and later, Renoir's cause was championed by major figures in French film culture who nurtured and disciplined the growth of young *cinéphilia*. At the Paris Cinémathèque, Henri Langlois lost no opportunity to screen Renoir's films and to set them among cinema's greatest and most educative achievements. The critic André Bazin, through his zeal and intellectual passion, spread the conviction that Renoir was the most vital figure in the French contribution to world cinema. His impact was all the greater because he was at the same time fostering the development of the new generation of critics – among them Truffaut – who were to gather round the monthly *Cahiers du cinéma* and quite soon to form the core of the New Wave of film-makers.

To acclaim Renoir's achievement was also necessarily to defend it against attack, since he had enemies on the left as well as on the right. His standing in many French eyes was compromised by his failure to return from America – from Hollywood! – after the German surrender. It was ten years before he made another film in the French studios, and in fact California remained his home until his death in 1979. His choice worried even his friends; it was open to a range of interpretations, many of them offensive to French sensibilities. The heat of cultural warfare did its bit to inflame the fervour of Renoir's admirers.

In that context, the absence of an authentic version of *La Règle du jeu* must have become, by 1956, worse than teasing. The directors of a Paris ciné-club set out to establish a more complete edition. They formed La Société des Grands Films Classiques, acquired the rights and assembled every scrap of film or negative they could lay hands on. Buoyed by their discovery of salvaged material in another laboratory – more than two hundred cans of it – Jean Gaborit and Jacques Maréchal worked with the editor Jacques Durand to reconstitute Renoir's movie. They went beyond restoration of the first premiere version to achieve something close to the 113 minutes that

Renoir had initially sanctioned. Although the term did not exist in 1959, their edition of *La Règle du jeu* was surely the first and still the most glorious instance in cinema history of a Director's Cut.

By eloquent coincidence the restored film had its festival screening in the season that found the French New Wave in glory at Cannes. As he was at Venice in 1959 to present his new film, *Le Testament du Docteur Cordelier*, Renoir was able to savour the rediscovery. 'Quite a triumph,' he wrote to his son Alain.[13] In *Sight & Sound*, Penelope Houston reported that 'on the day these two productions … were shown, the festival was unmistakably Renoir's'.[14]

André Bazin did not live to see this vindication. He died at forty in November 1958 before he could complete his book on Renoir. (In homage, Truffaut undertook to organise the manuscript and fill it out for publication.) One of the last acts of his life as a critic must have been to cast his votes, alongside those of Chabrol, Godard, Rivette, Rohmer and Truffaut among others, in the selection of

Alain Renoir, an assistant, on set with his father

Cahiers du cinéma's Twelve Best Films of All Time. *La Règle du jeu* was placed at the head, second only to Murnau's *Sunrise* (1927). The list was published in the issue for December 1958, which carried the announcement of Bazin's death.

Like the *Cahiers* vote, all Bazin's writing on *La Règle du jeu* must have been based on truncated prints. Yet he acclaimed the picture's brilliant construction and provided understandings of its achievement that have proved doubly seminal. Bazin illuminated *La Règle du jeu* in ways to which all subsequent criticism is indebted; he was also the first to insist on its centrality for our assessment of the cinema as a whole. Since then, everyone who presents a significant argument on the aesthetics of film has been obliged to take account of Renoir's work and to engage with Bazin's view of it.

The dedication to Bazin's memory was indeed a fitting tribute. But the opening announcement was not the only addition that Gaborit and Durand made to the resurrected movie. *La Règle du jeu* had always carried in its titles a disclaimer offering the picture as a *divertissement* and denying any ambitions as social criticism. In 1959, assuredly with Renoir's approval and most likely at his suggestion, the disclaimer was modified and subtly transformed by an addition that gave the film the character of a prophetic period piece. It now reads – italics mark the insert – as follows: 'This entertainment, *whose action occurs on the eve of the 1939 war*, makes no claim to be a study of manners. Its characters are pure make-believe.'

The inserted words were not put in to explain anything about the film's plot for an audience that would now be offered it under the rubric of Les Grands Films Classiques. They were there to alert the spectator to the purpose of *La Règle du jeu*, and to insist on the relevance of the eve-of-war context even though – or especially because – the process of national and international events would not intrude upon the action and would be absent from the concerns of the characters. Evoking the brink of war gave the author's approval to interpretations that emphasised social criticism. These new words asked that the film be seen in the light of the events that followed 1939. Thereby they prepared it for understanding as a portrait of the ruling class in its decadence, and as an analysis whose insights had been validated by the French collapse before Nazism.

There is an oddity, on the face of it, in making so much of the 1939 setting while retaining the surrounding words that seem to boast of insignificance. The stress on make-believe in the main text echoed the subtitle that, right at the start, identified *La Règle du jeu* as a 'dramatic fantasia' – with the French word *fantaisie* carrying the sense of the whimsical, of a caprice. The apparent contradiction here continues the dividedness that had marked Renoir's project since its inception. While still at the planning stage, he had told a journalist on *Pour Vous* that the film would offer 'a precise description of the bourgeoisie of our time'.[15] From a director who was also celebrated as an internationalist, anti-fascist and polemicist for the left, such an undertaking could only imply a denunciation; the description would predictably be merciless. On the other hand, he was setting out to make a comedy, of a sort, in a baroque spirit, drawing on French theatrical tradition, and offering himself and his audience a break from the warfare of *La Grande Illusion* (1937) and *La Marseillaise* (1937), and the murderous convulsions of *La Bête humaine* (1938).

The first and last of those films had been hugely successful, paving the way for Renoir to set up his own production company so as to work with greater freedom. It was hoped that La Nouvelle Édition Française would develop into a French counterpart to United Artists in the USA, offering independence to major French film-makers and allowing them to participate more fully in the rewards of success. But first it needed to prove itself at the box office. Renoir had established the NEF with a group of friends and associates. Did any of them remark that *La Grande Illusion* and *La Bête humaine* had both profited from the charismatic brilliance of Jean Gabin in the starring role, and that *La Règle du jeu* was going ahead – once Simone Simon had priced herself out of the female lead – without that kind of support?

We know that objections were raised when Renoir ended the search for a principal actress with an invitation to the all-but-unknown Nora Gregor, a refugee from Hitler's Austria. He was able to override the objections and to redirect his development of the scenario with this actress in mind. Gregor was to play Christine, wife of a French aristocrat and the centre of a tangle of amorous intrigue. Since Renoir's design was evolving towards an ensemble piece with a growing array of developed characters, he may well have felt that beyond his personal attraction to Gregor there was also an objective justification for non-star casting.

It was the strength of Renoir's position as the creative force in the NEF that he could insist on an artistic decision, or possibly a whim, in face of his associates' worries. But the strength contained some familiar weaknesses. The independent film author has no immediate source of financial discipline (such as a producer or a studio ordinarily imposes) to restrain the perfectionism that is necessary to the director's function. That would be a pure advantage, creatively, if the material resources were limitless. Since they never can be, the pursuit of the ideal may soon – as the costs pile up – put the artist back in thrall to the bankers.

Renoir was never a profligate film-maker, and he was conscious that his own money, as well as that of his friends, was riding on the success of the NEF. Still, there were corners that could not be cut. His story was of the idle rich in French society. It moved from Paris to the chateau of La Colinière for a shooting party, where a wealthy host spent freely for the entertainment of his many guests. On location, the weather was hostile and a two-week schedule stretched to five, leaving the sound stages at the Joinville studio expensively idle. There Eugène Lourié had constructed sets for the scenes inside the chateau based on a plan which would allow Renoir's camera to travel freely between spaces. This would enable the director to stage the action in ways that would stress not only luxury but also the continuity between conflicting interests, as well as the criss-crossing between the affairs of the masters and those of the servants.

La Ferté Saint-Aubin becomes … La Colinière

Rain on location ... and in the studio

Lourié's main set spread across both the largest sound stages. As the shooting extended beyond the initial eight-week schedule, the NEF came under pressure to release the space. Then some principal members of the cast, essential to scenes or shots that remained to be filmed, found themselves up against their commitments to other productions. Some of them had to go – Roland Toutain, for instance, to Morocco – and their uncertain availability became another hazard for the director. During a production hiatus when three scenes at the start of the movie remained to be shot, Renoir reflected on his experience in a letter to his NEF partner Camille François. He affirmed his belief in the film's quality but was not confident about its reception. Any problems, he wrote on the first day of June 1939, would be the result of circumstances that had

delayed the script of La Règle du jeu and made us start out with an incomplete draft. This draft wasn't good; I had to do several revisions during the shooting, and if La Règle du jeu is not well received by the public I think we must attribute it to that alone. It's a lesson for next time: we must never again start without being thoroughly prepared.[16]

Extensive overhauls to the screenplay after the start of production seem to have occurred only on those of Renoir's pictures where intractable problems drove him into panic. But it was part of his customary working method to embrace discoveries made in the course of rehearsal and shooting, and to adjust the film's development to the character of the settings and to the specific talents of the actors. Indeed it was the refusal to blueprint the detail of the movie's realisation that was to run him into conflict with governing concepts of efficiency during his career in the Hollywood studios. Part of the special richness of La Règle du jeu should perhaps be attributed to circumstances that pushed Renoir into a more extreme version of his normal practice.

It seems certain that the anxieties and tensions surrounding the production interacted with the wider context of life in 1939 to amplify

Preparing the shot with Nora Gregor and Jean Renoir

the movie's sense of the precarious, of barely containable hysteria. After the collapse of the Popular Front, the left in France was fractured in defeat. No one knew whether or how the arrest of fascism's triumph in Europe could be achieved. For most, a war was too dreadful to contemplate. Its horrors would multiply the carnage of 1914–18 by the new terrors of air attack that Hitler had demonstrated through his intervention in the Spanish Civil War. In the months of shooting on *La Règle du jeu*, between January and June 1939, it became ever more difficult to sustain the blind euphoria that had greeted the Munich Agreement. It required an ever more earnest investment of will to believe that the policy of appeasement would succeed in averting disaster – but many people in France and England were making that investment.

At various times, Renoir gave conflicting accounts of what he expected as the film was readied for its premiere. Speaking at the Academy Cinema in London in 1967, he recalled having been 'sure the public would like it – it was a light picture, parties are not big problems and the big problems were so well hidden that the audience wouldn't be hurt in their feelings. Well, I was very wrong.'[17] His autobiography repeats this theme. Yet his remarks in a radio broadcast on the day of the 1939 opening reflected the doubts expressed to Camille François: 'I'm anxious about the reception the public will accord to *La Règle du jeu*. But I believe it's an experience which is worth the trouble of attempting.'[18]

The contradictions became more pronounced when he discussed the film's content and intentions. In the Academy Cinema lecture, he denied a social purpose: 'People thought that … I was criticising society, but not at all. I wish I could live in such a society – that would be wonderful.' Introducing the film for French television four years later, his claim was reversed:

I wanted to … criticize a society that I considered to be rotten and that I continue to consider to be absolutely rotten, because this society is still the same. It's still rotten. It hasn't finished drawing us into some very pretty little catastrophes.[19]

No doubt it was not only the adjustment of memory to various occasions and purposes that left us these changing accounts but also the storyteller's drive to give his stories dash and colour, and the performer's judgment of what will keep the audience hanging on his words. Like many another great film-maker, Renoir was a beguiling conversationalist whose joy was to hold forth for the delight and instruction of his fellows. Whatever the qualifications advanced by the revisionists, Renoir's differing tales seem to me to be valuable as images even when they are less sure as history. They give convincing expression to ranges of feeling about the film and its production. A 1952 statement in *Cahiers du cinéma* suggests the difference between creative determination and intellectual uncertainty:

When I made *La Règle du jeu* I knew the way to go ... My instinct guided me. Awareness of danger provided me with situations and lines, and my comrades were in the same state as I. How troubled we were. I think the film is good.

Renoir introduces *La Règle du jeu* for French TV (1961)

But it's not so very hard to do good work with a compass of anxiety to guide your path.[20]

The contradictions in Renoir's accounts point up real tensions that are vital to the work's character. His autobiography tells us that during the shoot he was 'torn between the desire to make a comedy of it and the wish to tell a tragic story. The result of this ambivalence was the film as it is.'[21] We may take these words to represent the film-maker's understanding of his achievement, arrived at over a span of thirty years. 'Ambivalence' has to be a key term in any discussion of the film. I doubt too if any one phrase better evokes the instability of genre and the complexity of tone in *La Règle du jeu* than Renoir's remark in 1966 that he had based the film on the expression 'dancing on a volcano'.[22]

2 André Jurieu (Roland Toutain)

I was deeply troubled ... and it seemed to me that one way of interpreting the world's state of mind at this time was precisely *not* to discuss the situation but rather to tell a lightweight tale. So I looked for inspiration in Beaumarchais, Marivaux, the classical authors, and in comedy.[23]

The opening credits of *La Règle du jeu* are accompanied by a Mozart overture. As they end, the screen is filled with a verse from an eighteenth-century comedy, Beaumarchais' *The Marriage of Figaro* (1784), hence also with a reference to Mozart's comic opera of 1786. At the start of this *fantaisie dramatique* – which the pre-release publicity had promoted as 'Un drame gai' – we seem to be offered escape into the attitudes and entertainments of the past. The overture adapts the first of Mozart's German Dances, KV605. Nowadays it sounds formal, even courtly, and undemandingly tuneful. Beaumarchais' verse chides the world for its impatience with the changeability of human affections; it argues that, as Love has wings, it must be meant to flit about. The poetic language is archaic and the formality of the verse pattern is matched to sentiments offered with less than complete seriousness. We have been put in the mood for elegant order, artifice and a concentration on pursuits of love among the fickle.

But the prologue closes. The screen fades to black. The music stops. On the fade-in, as the action begins, everything seems to be reversed. The last note of music gives way to a babble of voices, clamouring impenetrably. The image opens on a night scene with a technician in headphones attending closely to the dials and meters on an electronic control panel. Behind him, in a shallow and confined space, a Radio-Cité board identifies his work with the operations of a broadcast station. The camera pulls back and tilts down to take in a

heavy reel turning as cable is unwound by the hands of an imperfectly
focused and insecurely framed workman. A female voice asserts itself
above the racket of the crowd with 'Radio-Cité calling ...'
The camera floats to the right, following the extension of the cable,
to discover in close-up a commentator. In the foreground, she grips a
bulky, barely portable, microphone – big enough to obscure her face
as she struggles to keep control of it while she pushes her way with
and through the mob. She is at Le Bourget airport, she says, to relay
the scene: a French aviator, André Jurieu, is about to complete a solo
flight across the Atlantic.

    The stress is on interruption. We are plunged into a world in
motion. The narrative has started, but nothing else has a beginning.
No stately exposition slows the world's processes. (This will be a
movie for the quick-witted. We shall need stamina to keep pace with
it. We may need several viewings to develop the stamina.) The major
happening – Jurieu's arrival – is the finish of an action, but not

evidently the start of anything. The commentator may open her report but we discover her in the middle of events; the technician was already engaged with whatever it was that he could hear.

We have gone from Mozart and Beaumarchais to a distinctly modern world of competing energies and of an ever-changing machinery of transport and communications. The airport, the radio, the live broadcast and the career woman are emblems of the up to date for 1939. Specifically for the French audience of the day, Radio-Cité, a popular station established as recently as 1935, was a new but familiar feature of daily life; and in the role of the commentator, Renoir had given a face to Radio-Cité's star reporter, Lise Elina.[24]

Key tokens of the contemporary are present in the background elements as well – noise, the illuminated night and the modern mob not of the dispossessed but of middle-class consumers of celebrity and the grand spectacle. These all act to destabilise the image and to extend an ambiguous prospect, the promise of freedom and the threat of chaos. You could join the mob and be carried in its surge. You could just as easily get trampled under its mass. As the plane comes in to land, the crowd breaks through the police cordon erected around the airstrip. The excited commentator expects her listeners to approve when she boasts that she too is pushing through.

The opening shot introduces techniques that we shall encounter through the film: the wandering camera apparently carried by the flow of action, and its counterpart the artful image of the spontaneous, crafted to suggest that happenstance holds sway. See how Renoir gives the impression that we are caught in the middle of the crowd's movement when, on his set, the size of the camera and the machinery of its transport require a clear foreground. He first establishes the turbulence of the image by moving without evident design, and through two changes of direction, from the technician down to the unreeling spool and across to the reporter. Then, he holds close to the reporter's face to put us in the middle of a crowd that in reality existed only to one side of the camera. The smoothly

governed movement of the camera itself is disguised by haphazard
lighting and by having the actress jostled so that her struggle to gain
ground is made vivid by the instability of her image within the frame.
Because she clutches the microphone in the hand nearest the camera,
another unsteady shape occupies the foreground. Only at the very
end of the shot, and briefly, do other figures intervene between the
actress and the camera as she appears to be swept away in the
onward rush.

The first cut inserts a shot of the taxiing aircraft. The montage
sets out as it means to go on – bluntly – not matching the angle on the
aeroplane to the commentator's upward glance and not fusing the
main directions of movement between one shot (the surging crowd)
and the one that follows (the aircraft). So it does without the visual
links that most film editors prize as an aid to elegant flow.
Elaborately sustained continuities within the shots are offset by the
jolt with which one image abuts on the next.

This method of cutting gives stylistic expression to two kinds of cross-purposes – those that weave a pattern, or tangle, and those that collide and jar. Cross-purpose is a large part of what this scene will be about, and an even larger factor in the way it will feel. While they are giving us information that will be basic to the plot, the words of the commentator do not seem like an exposition because the opening has so effectively plunged us into the drama of making this transmission from this place now. The story seems to be about the work of broadcasters rather than about the subject of their broadcast. We have been given a quick and vivid insight into the reporter's aims and priorities, and could be forgiven for assuming that she will be a main character in *La Règle du jeu*.

But the aviator will not collude in the designs of Radio-Cité and its servants. They want a story of resolve, endurance and triumph: the nation's hero receives the nation's welcome. The man from the ministry is there to extend official recognition and, of course, to have some of the glory rub off on the politicians he represents. At first it all meshes nicely. André Jurieu blears about him under the flashlights and has understandable difficulty in connecting with the scene. But he accepts the minister's congratulations with becoming modesty; he even does the good prize-winner's bit about teamwork. Then matters take an unlooked-for turn. He glances off screen away from the bureaucrat and his face lights up as he recognises an old pal, Octave. The hugs and smiles of greeting between friends carve out a space of intimacy. Responding to this shift away from his public role, Jurieu undoes the strap of his flying helmet so that we see more of his face, less of his uniform. He turns serious and poses the question that matters to him most: 'She's here?'

No sooner has Octave's dejected reply wiped the smile from the pilot's face than the woman from Radio-Cité approaches, pressing for a few words for the listeners. André's dismay and the urgency of his need for explanation make him oblivious to her appeals and then impatient with them. The image measures the clash of purposes by having the microphone-wielder insert herself head-on, a bit out of

focus, between the facing profiles of the aviator and his friend.
On the soundtrack, her attempt to grasp an interview jars against
Jurieu's questions to Octave. His need to know how and why his lady
has failed him is deadlocked against the announcer's need to obtain a
moment of intimacy with the hero. Persisting, she thrusts herself
between the two friends and pushes Octave aside, out of the frame.

It is not clear who is the intruder here. It could be Octave;
his indifference to the public aspects of what is after all a big public
occasion could mean that he is more out of place than the woman.
Each of them is discountenanced in their different ways when Jurieu's
frustration leads him to explode the distinction between the private
and the public. He crouches forward to shout into the microphone,
as if into the face of the absentee: 'I've never before been so let down.
I took on this challenge entirely because of a woman. She isn't even
here to see me. She couldn't be bothered. If she's listening I tell her
publicly she has betrayed me.'

Exhausted and in distress, Jurieu treats the OB mike like a telephone, issuing to all the world a private message whose intimacy he guards – despite that 'publicly' – by withholding the lady's name. If the actual and the implied technologies of distant communication both assert the modernity of the film's world, André seems to have turned back the clock on aviation to convert his solo flight into a knightly quest, performed to show him worthy of a lady's favour.

Perhaps he has overdone the courtly aspect, since this lady too is a married woman. Jurieu will enlist his friend Octave's aid in order to resume the pursuit. In the denouement, Octave's efforts will result in a fatal misunderstanding and Jurieu's death. This basic structure, and the pattern of relationship between a lovelorn melancholic and his libertine friend, is the clearest trace in the film of its debt to *Les Caprices de Marianne*, the Alfred de Musset play of 1833 that Renoir acknowledged as the basis of his tale. The film starts with the two characters most closely derived from Musset's leading pair of Neapolitans, Octavio (now Octave) and Celio, who has become André Jurieu. It will straightway present us with Musset's eponymous heroine in the guise of Christine, the wife of the Marquis Robert de La Chesnaye, and the object of Jurieu's desire.

While Jurieu has the excuse of exhaustion after a thirty-six-hour solo flight, he has been swift to turn his triumph into a disaster. The hero has become an embarrassment for whom excuses will need to be made. He may be young enough and reasonably good-looking but he could hardly present an initial impression more removed from the norm for the doomed lover. We can usually tell all too clearly when a character is being prepared for a tragic death. The film will do everything to present an image of appealing vulnerability. Not here. It is one of the most challenging features of *La Règle du jeu* that while it organises its narrative round André's pursuit of Christine, it goes out of its way to prevent us from making an emotional investment in the success or failure of the courtship. Renoir develops romantic conflicts without declaring whether any of their possible resolutions should make us happy or sad.

When he gets over his petulance, André will turn out to be mildly likeable. He is certainly not detestable, which would give the film another way to direct the flow of feeling. No, his is precisely a neither one thing nor the other personality. Within the array of the film's characters, and their distinct types of colourful individuality, Jurieu is the epitome of ratherness. Start to imagine Jean Gabin in the role and you realise the weightlessness of André's presence. He is weightless even in death, since his cadaver does not earn the camera's interest.

Roland Toutain enjoyed big success early in the sound era before finding his niche in uniformed parts. He was enough of a celebrity to publish his autobiography – *Mes quatre cents coups* – in 1951. By that account he had, off screen even more than on, a flamboyant career as a trapezist, professional daredevil and airborne stuntman. *La Règle du jeu* was by no means the first movie to present him in the guise of a pilot. Of his starring debut in 1930 Toutain writes, 'In *Le Mystère de la chambre jaune* I created the character I like best, since it's got everything I aspire to: movement, gaiety, acrobatics with a smiling face – few lines to speak – everything I like.'[25] Little wonder that his book makes just one passing reference to *La Règle du jeu*. It seems that Renoir must have cast him in order to strip away everything that audiences had come to expect. Memories of the other Toutains would then work to suggest that movement, gaiety and the smiling face had all been banished by disappointment in love. That could mean also that the audience of the day would have been expecting, and eager, to see buoyancy regained.

But the character remains morose, resourceless and self-pitying. Octave's devotion is apparent and infectious. It provides our main reason to feel that an André recovered from his lovesickness could be a man to enjoy. Renoir could have chosen to begin the movie at an earlier stage in Jurieu's enterprise. Then he would have been able to give us a colourful André, and to involve us in the plans, hopes and fears leading to his success. But starting with the completion of the exploit does more to establish the aviator's fame than to enlist our sympathy or admiration. In any case, the Atlantic crossing was no longer a feat to compare with Lindbergh's; that – the Radio-Cité commentator reminds us – was twelve years in the past. The year 1939 marked the beginning of Pan-American Airways' regular commercial service between Europe and America. France had lost its leading role in the development of aviation, and there was every reason for anxiety over questions of air power. The mob fervour that greets Jurieu's success suggests a nervous readiness to affirm French heroism by investing a stunt with the glamour of triumph. Having himself been a flyer in World War I, with a wounded soldier's view of military pomp, Renoir is all the more likely to have felt this undercurrent, and wanted it.

The director was following his regular method in casting Toutain against type. He was always more concerned with the way an actor's being might impress itself on character and situation than with finding a performer who would sink himself into the preconceived requirements of the role. An actor's physique, voice and manners translate to the screen in strange ways – at best, to unique effect. And the impact of two or more such individualities framed together obeys no mathematical rule. At its highest levels, film direction requires acute intuition and great luck, as well as devious calculation, to make good use of the camera's interest in the variousness of human expression.

In giving us a floundering Toutain, an abject and blundering Jurieu, the film equips us to see Octave's point when he describes his friend as the typical hero of the modern world – spectacular in his mastery of an arcane skill but useless in the ordinary business of life. Octave will say this to his face, accusingly: 'You've got your head in the clouds. Take you out of your plane and you make a mess of everything.' Much later he will say the same thing to Christine, this time in André's defence:

You've got to understand him. He's just like all our modern heroes. Up in the skies they're terrific. As soon as they're back on the ground, it all drains away;

they're pathetic and helpless, as clumsy as toddlers. They can fly the Atlantic but they can't get across the Champs-Élysées in one piece.

André's death will not be the tragedy that some commentators want to see. It is another of his stumbles – a bit like a shot rabbit or pheasant – rather than a fall from a hero's height. Jurieu never imposes himself on the tale. A lot of the time he's scarcely active, close to invisible. When he gets his chances, he muffs them.

First off, he cannot manage a suicide. Suffering rejection, he does not care whether he lives or dies. At the wheel of a car, then, with Octave as passenger, he does not care that his driving could kill his terrified companion. He crashes into a ditch. The event is abruptly presented; nothing is done to create sympathy or to develop suspense about the outcome. Octave's fondness for André is such that shock and fury soon give way to the desire to relieve his friend's pain. Octave negotiates with both Christine and her husband, the Marquis Robert de La Chesnaye, and gets them to agree to invite Jurieu to the shooting party at Robert's chateau, La Colinière. The next time we see André is when he arrives at the mansion with Octave. The assembled guests are in a great but decorously controlled tizzy. The pilot is a hero of the day and the subject of exciting speculation: everyone is aware that Christine is the woman whose name he did not speak in his radio outburst, but no one is sure how intimate their previous relationship had been. What is common knowledge – to all but Christine – is that her husband has long been embroiled in an affair with the sophisticate, Geneviève de Marras, who is another guest on hand to witness Jurieu's entrance.

Everything is stewing up appetisingly for a big scene and we get it; but it is played almost entirely on Christine. Where André made a mess of his big occasion at Le Bourget, Robert's wife gives the perfect performance in this difficult spot. She introduces Jurieu to the company as a good friend whose exploit she is glad to have encouraged. With a speech that combines bravado and naive sincerity, she wins acclaim for her moment in the spotlight. André is an essential accessory to this occasion, but hardly its star, and he remains sidelined throughout the days and nights that follow. He is present to little effect in the major event of the hunt. We still have not seen him in – or even seeking – any private moment with Christine. He spends his time only with Octave and with Christine's niece Jackie, a wan and colourless little sort, a suitable match and in love with him, but defeatedly. Somewhere at the back of our feeling about Jurieu must be the sense that he prefers being unhappy in love. Why else would he hang around without making occasion to press his suit with Christine?

He is absent again at the drama's next turning point. In the hunt's aftermath, Christine learns of her husband's infidelity. Awareness of his long-standing deception, and of society's collusion in it, deranges her and inclines her towards an intrigue of her own. But in this mood she finds the thought of André's earnestness a turn-off. Everything comes to a head on the night of the big party with all of La Colinière *en fête*. Fancy dress and alcohol work together to loosen the ties of decorum. Jurieu is at last spurred to action when he sees Christine offering herself to a stiff prig called Saint-Aubin, whose interest in her is anything but romantic. André's action consists of deriding the aristocrat's challenge to a duel, and pointing up the derision by entering into a scrap, boxing his ears and kicking his backside. This is surprisingly inelegant and heart-warming. For Christine too, since she now turns round and declares her love. Again Jurieu does the wrong thing, a whole mess of wrong things. When Christine (as she later complains to Octave) wants her suitor to kiss her and make off with her, the best he can manage is to bring up questions of etiquette, to insist on talking things over with her husband and taking her to meet his mother. Alarmingly for Christine, his sexual appetite turns out to be less urgent than his sense of propriety.

André certainly does not deserve Christine. But then plenty of men get more than they deserve. Or less. Just as surely, André does not deserve to get killed. When he is gunned down, it comes from the

knot of other affairs and collusions and misunderstandings that has
been tying itself up in the chateau. Christine's maid Lisette has taken
a fancy to the new servant, Marceau, who was until recently a petty
thief poaching rabbits on the grounds of La Colinière. Her husband is
Schumacher, who has a gamekeeper's attitude – for that is what he is
– to anyone who thinks to poach his wife. So Schumacher is out in
the grounds after midnight, shotgun at the ready and inflamed by his

A bit of fun, an outraged husband; André explains the rules of adultery

wife's flightiness, when he thinks he sees Octave headed for a tryst with her in the little greenhouse. The Lisette he imagines is, as we know, Christine dressed in Lisette's cloak. After he has fired the one deadly shot, the gamekeeper discovers the other thing we already knew, the identity of his target. We had seen Octave, in an act of self-sacrifice, give up his own dream of romance and send André in his place to meet Christine.

Jurieu's death is, fittingly, the culmination of a host of follies, disguises and misperceptions. It is also the last result of his habit of doing the wrong thing in the wrong place at the wrong time. So I think we should not rush to agree with the view that Renoir propounded in the years after the film's restoration. He was fond of picturing André as a ritual sacrifice, who had had to come to grief on account of the essential purity that made him an alien presence in a society of the impure.[26] Gauche, naive and by his own lights well meaning, Jurieu can often seem. But if these constitute purity, then Jurieu has no monopoly. What does single him out is his lack of force and colour. His voice particularly lacks personality. If he is an alien presence at La Colinière, it is more because – though he dies like one – he is the least rabbit-like figure on the premises, the one with the least animal vigour. Think back to the costumes for the fete. They all seem to fit the character of the wearer by heightening some particular trait as, most obviously, Octave's disguise as a bear declares an affable clumsiness that he struggles to shed. But André? What is he supposed to be? He carries a whip. He wears what might be a gypsy headdress and since he keeps on whipping the Octave-bear's behind, he is presumably its master. But all the gestures are feeble, and the whip and headscarf are mere ornaments over evening dress with black tie and costume trousers. With freedom to invent, Jurieu still could not find himself a character.

3 Robert de La Chesnaye (Marcel Dalio)

The stage is set for the last act of the tragedy. I am of a mind to let it begin …
I long to break out of this false situation … [put] an end to this sinister
comedy. (Marie Antoinette in *La Marseillaise*)

For the ordinary man it's a terrible thing to die in war. For men like us
it's a good way out. (De Boeldieu to Rauffenstein, his enemy friend, in *La
Grande Illusion*)

Robert de La Chesnaye is remarkable for his poise and
inventiveness in dealing with awkward situations, and for the pride
he takes in his ability to glide through the social world apparently
unshaken – even to some degree amused – by the nasty surprises it
can deliver. Of course, it helps that he is unimaginably rich.
When you look at the properties he owns and the staff he employs,
his wealth is evident and enormous. What we never see is the means
by which this wealth is generated or sustained. Since he gives every
appearance of being accustomed to living in luxury, and since no
one ever mentions what he does to earn his living, we can assume
that Robert relies on his inheritance to maintain his position among
the idle rich. (It is not long before we learn that he is a marquis,
which places him in the ranks of the nobility between the dukes and
the counts.)

The last thing we hear about him, practically the last line in the
film, is 'La Chesnaye is not without class.' This verdict is spoken by
the bluff old general who serves both as the arbiter and the mourner
of upper-class decorum. It is his appraisal of the marquis' behaviour
under the most testing circumstances, when Robert has succeeded in
putting an acceptable gloss on the slaughter of Jurieu. Standing on
the steps of the chateau, La Chesnaye is in an exposed position as he

addresses the audience beneath him, a jury of guests assembled in their dressing gowns and drawn out into the night air by the sound of a shot, the rumour of a killing. But he finds serviceable words and appropriate sentiments, managing both the necessary warmth in speaking of Jurieu and the necessary formality in offering an explanation of the 'deplorable accident'. His control is manifest in long sentences imbued with emotion but elegantly shaped and perfect in syntax.

The strategic, formally decisive, contrast is with Jurieu's performance at the start of the film. Called upon for a public accounting at Le Bourget, Jurieu turns triumph to disaster and lets everyone down, himself most of all, by blurting out unpalatable truths. At the end, in the face of catastrophe and under manifest if unspoken pressure, La Chesnaye does the reverse. He comes up with a performance that hides embarrassing facts behind a screen of plausible invention. At the start, Jurieu's failure to carry off his role

Robert faces his jury

has to be excused by the radio commentator; at the end, La Chesnaye's success is recognised in the general's praise.

There are powerful similarities in the image to heighten the contrasts between the two scenes. In both, the action takes place out of doors and at night; darkness and artificial light give the basic visual tone in each case. But the two characters with whom the movie began – André and Octave – are absent from its finale,[27] and the noise, crush and turmoil of the start have been replaced by order, distance and stately movement. Backing the speech is music, not Mozart here but elegantly plaintive strains from the French baroque (an arrangement of an entr'acte from Monsigny's 1769 opera *Le Déserteur*). For the first time since the action began, it is accompanied by music presented unambiguously as a device of the film's rather than as an aspect of the setting. It plays steadily throughout the final scenes, underlining their pathos but also enhancing the sense of artifice.

All the intimations of theatre and archaic form carried by the verse and the music at the film's preamble, so immediately contradicted by the opening action, now reach their fulfilment. From the chaos of the airport we have been brought to a relic of the *ancien régime*, with Robert urging his wife and guests to get some sleep within. The familiar steps at the chateau's entrance are presented in an image of pronounced symmetry and, not for the first time, they have the look and function of a stage. As the guests re-enter the building after the general's final words, we see them as shadows cast across the façade. In silhouette, the line of boxed yews below the balustrade evokes the image of footlights. Presented at the sober end of the night's madness, this *envoi* is distinctly imbued with the sense that our Prospero has declared the end of the revels. But the movement to leave the stage is also, as we see it from the outside, a retreat into the shelter of the old mansion's light and warmth.

The emphasis on theatricality has a dual movement. In one direction it affirms the continuing validity of traditional forms, and the power of creative fancy to move us and show us things that matter. As an image of the state of affairs at the drama's end, however, theatricality represents a defeat and a submission to paralysis. The characters have become set within the artifice that they had seemed freely to adopt and exploit. Elegance has been drained of anything true or useful, so that the forms that once served as modes of authentic expression are now at best the means to secure a regime of hypocrisy. Early in the film, Christine had remarked that 'a lie is a very heavy cloak to wear', but now we see the whole community colluding to accept the burdens of falsehood.

So Robert's success is also his failure. The retreat within the walls of La Colinière represents the defeat of his aspiration to freedom and fluidity. Agreeing to include Jurieu among the guests, he had proclaimed himself to be an enemy of walls and barriers. Almost as soon as he arrived at the chateau, in a move parallel to one that extends hospitality to his wife's suitor, he found himself inviting Marceau the poacher to join the staff of the estate. This is in line with his refusal to protect the grounds from rabbits by erecting wire

netting. But recruiting the poacher goes a good way beyond the purely negative, if unattainable, desire for an absence of both fences and rabbits.

It is presumably the marquis' appetite for inclusion that leads him to accede to the poacher's desire for a job *inside* the chateau. We do not see the moment of decision, but we have seen La Chesnaye beguiled both by Marceau's calling and by his manner. The little thief confides his yen to wear a servant's uniform. Such perversity amuses Robert and attracts his condescension. Besides, adding this human curio to his retinue must come easily to one with his passion for collecting. The gamekeeper is upset to see the master extending patronage to the poacher. He suffers under the clarity of Robert's demonstration that to bend the rules of property is the ultimate expression and privilege of ownership.

La Chesnaye's wish for an estate free from both barriers and intruders reflects his hankering for a world without hard choices and painful consequences. Though the decor of his residences both in town and country shows the range of his collecting interests, the one most actively in evidence is his passion for elaborate mechanical toys with complex but reliably musical action. As far as Robert is concerned, the highlight of the festivities at La Colinière will be the unveiling of his most recent acquisition of a *limonaire*, a huge fairground organ with 'live' percussion executed by the figurines that decorate its façade. His pride in these automatons when they work, and his agitation when they fail, projects his fantasy of himself as the master of ceremonies in a perfectly regulated world.

An ideal represented by command over antique but functioning clockwork is at odds with the dream of a world where everyone speaks and acts freely. The two can be reconciled only in a further fantasy, an 'if only'. Robert's longing is for a world without conflict, where people are happy to remain fixed in the stations – social or romantic – that best suit his convenience and his fancy. Being sharp enough to see that happiness would depend on their doing so freely, he imagines a regime in which, for instance, women would not suffer

at being disposed of according to his immediate sexual or domestic appetites. (He calls this the 'Muslim' way.) For all that he suffers from the world's refusal to work like this, it is not clear that he can ever face up to the root conflict between his notions of freedom and his concerns for property and the status quo.

Robert is, in a strict sense, irresponsible. He likes to say yes and in key decisions – about his mistress as well as over Jurieu and Marceau – he trusts to luck, recklessly, that no harm will come of it. In the poacher's case, he is not even asked for a decision. Marceau is caught trespassing and red-handed – rabbit-handed – by Schumacher, and is naturally elated when the lord of the manor takes his side. With his first words, Marceau makes it plain that he is one who cannot safely be given an inch. But he turns to the marquis with a seducer's confiding flattery. La Chesnaye is hooked, and immediately enters onto terms of intimacy with him.[28]

Marceau is an entertainer who comes along when Robert is at a loose end. Recently arrived at La Colinière and listlessly surveying his estate, the marquis presents the picture of a city man always threatened by boredom but now cut off from the city's amusements. Marceau, on the other hand, is a rogue who is wriggling his way through life by providing diversion and laughter. A boisterous extrovert, he gets by on cheek, colourful speech and extravagantly vivid gesture. He even makes a performance out of walking.

We can see what charms La Chesnaye in the character of Marceau because we are deriving similar delight from the actor – a Renoir favourite – Julien Carette.[29] It would have been easy for the acting to become monotonous in a movie largely populated with characters whose social roles confine them to contained gesture and correct speech. Carette/Marceau is a vital resource for Renoir in averting this threat. Though the character is one versed in country ways, the role is played with a strong accent from the streets of Paris. The hand and arm gestures, especially, are a stream of invention –

A Renoir favourite: Carette in *La Bête humaine*

coarse, vigorously contorted, and projected as if to reach the far corners of a music hall. They carry a welcome flavour of indecency.

As a figure of low theatre, a mechanical, Marceau falls within a recognisable tradition in being short, a bit of a runt. But his lack of inches is also one of the ways in which he resembles the marquis. They are similar in height, build and colouring. During the fete and even more on the occasion of their first meeting, their costumes are matched so that Marceau can seem like La Chesnaye's unrefined reflection.

With his contempt for all that is correct, Marceau gives rein to everything that Robert cannot allow himself. The marquis should hardly be amazed to see the ex-poacher erupt into the routines of bourgeois festivity as the very spirit of mayhem. In the chain of circumstance that will produce Jurieu's death, Marceau's comical flirtation with the gamekeeper's wife is a crucial link. At one point amid the stresses of the big party, Marceau becomes something like the confidant that Robert lacks, someone with whom to exchange

A matched pair

problems, advice and commiseration. Drawn by his envy of Marceau's carnal, scruple-free and apparently effective approach to women, La Chesnaye finds himself entering into the service of his servant, colluding with him to outwit Schumacher.

We might ask whether Robert fails to see the danger or whether he is perhaps drawn to it. Time and again in Renoir's work, people of privilege act out a suicidal bent that makes them invite destruction on themselves (*La Grande Illusion*) or their world (*La Marseillaise*). In going against the man he employs to look after his estate, and in giving his favour to a thieving reprobate, La Chesnaye is making a large gesture from on high. Again there are precedents throughout Renoir's work for strange liaisons that arise from the tendency of the grass to seem greener on the other side of a class divide. Remember *Boudu sauvé des eaux* (1932), most obviously. It is as if the man chafing under obligations of wealth and status gambles that he can import into his own world the freedom that he imagines in the lives of those at the bottom of the hierarchy. In this perspective, we can see that Robert virtually charges Marceau with the task of disruption that, in the event, he performs to excess.

One thing the marquis fails to consider is that a parasite owes no loyalty to its host. But he does not have to face, as we do, the least charming display of Marceau's opportunism. He becomes Schumacher's accomplice when he finds him set on killing Lisette's lover. It is Carette's remarkable achievement to make this turn of events both shocking and completely plausible. Its effect is to remind us that we, like Robert, have preferred to be amused by Marceau's shamelessness and to ignore the dangers in his capacity for subservience and in his devotion to petty self-interest.

If La Chesnaye's dealings with Marceau have the look of a flirtation, his relationship with Schumacher seems more like a bad marriage. The gamekeeper is the one person in Robert's entourage to whom he is always happy to say no. After the hunt, Robert offers no word of praise or thanks for Schumacher's effective management of affairs, only an irritated rebuff to a suggestion about the display of

Antagonists … united

the day's bag. While he looks into Marceau's face as if into a flattering mirror, he can only briefly bring himself to look at Schumacher at all. He can see what fury the poacher incites, so when he yields to the impulse to give him a job it must be largely for the fun of vexing Schumacher.

The landlord who loves the poacher and despises the gamekeeper – these characterisations must be thematic. But Marceau and Schumacher are clearly also a version of the traditional duo, the comic antagonists from the lower orders. They are starkly contrasted, and almost every dimension of difference aligns Robert with Marceau in opposition to Schumacher. Like the marquis, Marceau loves talking, is intolerant of silence and unhappy when out of conversation. Schumacher's words are few and simple, mainly limited to seeking and giving orders.

Physically, gamekeeper and poacher are, in music-hall terms, the long and the short of it. Schumacher stands tall and rigid, always in soldierly uniform with his cap and high boots even when indoors. The noise of his tread announces him wherever he goes as one who means to be seen. Where his dress and bearing declare his devotion to order, they also play against the soft, trickly roundness of Marceau, to whom dodging, lurking and hiding come easily.

The severe features of Gaston Modot, another Renoir favourite,[30] help to suggest the pained stoicism of a man impelled by duty rather than by any hope of happiness, a harsh observer of the world's corruption, quick and unyielding in his judgment of the flimsiness he sees all around. Encased in his uniform, he would be hard and cold to the touch, and he carries with him the chilly dampness of the Sologne marshes. His lips are thin, not made for smiling. He has a dead stare that most readily projects disapproval and frustration. Fixed in misery, he lacks both generosity and a sense of proportion.

In appearance as well as personality, he has much in common with the sadistic, jealously scheming valet Joseph, as played by Francis Lederer in Renoir's *Diary of a Chambermaid* (1946).

Although its fulfilment was long delayed, an ambition to film Octave Mirbeau's 1900 novel had engaged Renoir long before he started work on *La Règle du jeu*, and it is clear that Mirbeau's sardonic maid's-eye view of upper-class corruption had an abiding influence. The dark, sour presence of the novel's Joseph hangs over some of the detail and most of the mood of the film's Schumacher.

As the misanthropic butt of the film's licensed clown, Schumacher is also unmistakably in the mould of Shakespeare's Malvolio. Here, as in *Twelfth Night*, the figure of gloom and censure is treated with a troubling callousness that soon turns to cruelty. The first we hear of him is in Paris, where the marquis makes fun of a letter sent from La Colinière in which, we gather, Schumacher has complained of the loneliness caused by his wife Lisette's prolonged absence in the service of the marquise. Our first taste of Robert's snobbery comes with the amusement he derives from this letter.

Modot, between Dalio and Carette with Jean Dasté in *La Grande Illusion*

Once the host and guests arrive at the chateau, misery accumulates for Schumacher. He has first to put up with his wife's indifference, then with being thwarted by La Chesnaye's indulgence of the poacher, then with Lisette's feelingless rejection of his gift when she laments the lack of style in the cloak he has bought her. It is hardly any time after this that he finds Lisette on the floor of the servants' hall giggling as she is cuddled by Marceau.

It is representative of the film's method that the figure easiest to dislike, and the one who does the most harm, should also be the one most put upon and ultimately the character whose pain is made most vivid to us. *La Règle du jeu* is set against the moral stinginess that Schumacher displays. Necessarily then, it treats him with generosity; it shows the provocations under which he acts; it maintains, for him almost uniquely, a clear and consistent line of motivation.

The gamekeeper's consistency is, however, largely a product of his narrowness of view, the unthinking certainty with which he regards an equivocal world. Could this be a reaction to insecurity?

Joseph and the chambermaid (Paulette Goddard) in *Diary of a Chambermaid*

The first time we hear his name, we are immediately reminded that its origins are German, not French, and that it is more correctly pronounced with a German accent. (Within the same minute, we hear from his wife that she would rather divorce him than change the job that keeps them apart.) Later we learn that Schumacher comes from Alsace, a region which had been part of Germany for the forty years before 1919. In his initial fury at Marceau, the gamekeeper makes a remark that will become germane at the film's end. When he protests that it ought to be legal to fire on such little swine, he tells us that he knows it is not. When he further proclaims that during the war he shot better chaps than Marceau, it is worth noting that he would have done this shooting on the German side, not the French, and that he is complaining not of past injustice but of present laxity.

Schumacher regrets the lack of military discipline to order the world around him, and he is nostalgic for an Alsatian regime where

The gift of a cloak

'we know how to deal with poachers and scum like Marceau.
A well-aimed bullet at night in the woods and that's the last you hear
of them.' His conviction that disorder is the greatest of evils, and his
attachment to simple violent solutions, marks him as a presence of
lower-class fascism. His fellow servants take for granted his hostility
to foreigners and Jews. In these respects too, the character is a
descendant of Mirbeau's Joseph.

Schumacher is a more wholehearted upholder of hierarchy
and of the rights and obligations of ownership than his master.
He believes in putting up fences, and taking the gun equally to
rabbits, cats, trespassers and wife-poachers. Our sympathy for him
as the victim of Lisette's heartlessness is put in tension with our
awareness that he would make a miserable husband. Faced with the
failure of his attempt at courtship, he tries to assert his authority by
issuing petty orders that make his wife his drudge.

It is clear enough why Schumacher should harbour a silent
contempt for the marquis. Being himself without sophisticated

doubts, he is frustrated by aristocratic indecision, by the lack of strong leadership from the top. The conflicting values and temperaments of master and servant come to a final collision when Robert's assent to the dissolution of his marriage, sanctioning Jurieu's departure with Christine, criss-crosses with Schumacher's resolve to kill the man who offends against his ownership of Lisette.

When La Chesnaye sees in Marceau an image of enviable life, it is on the rebound from his dislike of Schumacher and his recoil from all that the gamekeeper represents. In his role and in his bearing, Schumacher shows with painful clarity the violence that upholds Robert's wealth and lifestyle. La Colinière's guests lean towards the belief that Schumacher was acting to order when he killed Jurieu. They are not quite right about that. However, when he developed the role of the gamekeeper, Renoir had to be conscious that his borrowings from Musset were putting Schumacher into a very particular place. In *Les Caprices de Marianne*, the Jurieu figure falls victim to assassins that the jealous husband has paid to ambush his wife's lover. Schumacher is Renoir's counterpart of these hired killers.

One of the key decisions Renoir made about the staging of the film's ending was to have Schumacher, gun across his back, on the steps alongside La Chesnaye as the words of explanation are spoken. Lighting and movement make both the figure and the weapon unmissable presences in the image. During the speech, the gamekeeper makes an unresolved shift that takes him nearer both to his employer and to the doors of the chateau, as if uncertain whether he is to join the stream of movement inside. What is sure, however, is that killing André has restored Schumacher to the job from which he had earlier been dismissed. His function and his innocence are necessary to the tale concocted to conceal the fact that Jurieu was shot in the course of eloping with Robert's wife.

The killer's reinstatement cannot be acknowledged. It has to be as if he was never paid off. But it is tacitly conveyed, to him and to us, when La Chesnaye instructs him to take charge of the accident scene. This exchange immediately follows a scene in which Octave and

Marceau say goodbye as each of them begins his journey of departure from the chateau. With Jurieu dead, Marceau cast out and Schumacher vindicated, La Chesnaye's experiment in openness has met with defeat.

The freedom that Robert yearns for has proved incompatible with the way of life he clings to. His position and his property require a Schumacher. La Chesnaye and the gamekeeper are the joint masters of the hunt, the event that provides the *raison d'être* for Robert's hospitality. This vile celebration of ownership is aptly described by Peter Wollen as 'the senseless destruction of natural beings in order to conform with a style of life'.[31]

Robert takes no delight in the hunt. For him it is interchangeable with any other festival of the high life – like a ski party. His pleasure is to provide entertainment for his friends and to uphold his place in society. He does this from a position of material security but without inner conviction. His life seems to be spent in pursuit of distraction, and organised on the assumption that it is his

Robert laments, Schumacher stands by

role to lay on distraction for others. When his mistress complains that his boredom has deadened their romance, she brings out something that has been visible since the first time we saw them. She also points to a more general understanding of La Chesnaye's case. To develop an obsession – for instance, as a collector of antique mechanisms – is one way of giving oneself something to do and making it feel important. It can greatly assist in the quest for an illusion of significance.

The concern with boredom is one of the keys to the desperation that informs *La Règle du jeu*. The dramatisation of boredom looks beyond the simply negative state of being without the means to occupy time. It presents it with its aspects of anger, resentment and futility as a tactic of evasion and with its consequences, in the hunt, of hardened brutality. With Robert, it appears as a fearful refusal – seemingly allied to a sense of impotence – to make the serious assessment of his life and its discontents that might entail radical thinking. Such a move cannot be made without the support of hope.

But there is more defeat than hope in Robert's bearing. He is without the self-confidence that ought to go with his position and his ability to rise to public occasions. He often seems conscious of his height, especially with his women – both of whom are considerably taller. He is given to apologetic gestures of impotence, shrugging his shoulders and flapping his arms. The giveaway is his actorly habit of wiping his mouth with his handkerchief, as if worried that his lips may carry some repulsive or ridiculous blemish. When he does this at the end of the picture, before checking Schumacher's arrangements for the corpse, it is one of several gestures that show how anxiously his mind is trained upon the presentational challenge ahead.

Looking back with Dalio in 1966, Renoir commented on the shot where La Chesnaye presents his *limonaire* ('the best I've ever done') and congratulated the actor on the 'mix of humility and pride, of triumph and uncertainty – nothing definite – underlying a lot of other stuff'.[32] In the same passage, Renoir comments on his reasons for casting Dalio and stresses the importance in such matters of going

Aids to acceptable appearance: a pocket mirror ... and a handkerchief

against the norm. Dalio's autobiography puts the matter more bluntly. He confesses to feeling out of place in the Sologne countryside, hints at strategic miscasting by Renoir, and wonders at the transformation required of 'Marcel Blauschild, aka Dalio' to have him emerge as a figure of the French aristocracy.[33]

Dalio's insecurity in his film role becomes La Chesnaye's insecurity in his social performance. Though the act is successful, we can see the effort that Robert puts into it. Once with his mistress and once with his wife, he confesses his fear of humiliation. Like many of us, the character carries with him a doubt about his standing in others' eyes, and he overcompensates. Dalio's Jewishness gives this aspect of the character an additional resonance. It is as if he is aware or fearful of remarks made behind his back that we find directly expressed only below stairs in whispers. Spiteful gossip across the servants' dinner table wants to make an issue of the fact that the boss's maternal grandfather was called Rosenthal[34] and came from Frankfurt.

Similar sentiments are capable of more oblique expression, however. A note of disdain is audible in the delivery of the general's final comment on Robert's *savoir faire* – 'Ce La Chesnaye ne manque pas de classe'. The general would never admit that he expects his listener to put quotation marks round the name and to collude in hearing an implied and derogatory 'Rosenthal'.

In 1939, Renoir took two great risks with the characterisation of La Chesnaye. One threat – fully realised in the film's reception – was of creating a hate-object for nationalists and anti-Semites. Marcel Dalio quotes some shameful words, including these from the right-wing *l'Action française*:

Dalio is astonishing, more Jewish than ever, attractive and squalid simultaneously ... He exudes a different odour from far back in time, of another race, always watchful, that does not hunt, owns no chateau, and to whom the Sologne means nothing. Never before perhaps had the alien character of the Jew been displayed with such force, such brutality.[35]

The other danger was more subtle. At the end of the movie, Robert is getting away with a pack of lies. The retreat into the chateau recognises that this cream of society exists in no useful relationship with the modernity depicted in the film's opening. Conviction and steadiness of purpose have turned out to be the prerogative of a thoughtless and murderous conformism. Throughout the picture, La Chesnaye is the chief representative of privilege in all its irresponsibility and condescension. In the atmosphere of the late 1930s, Robert's wealth and his decadence might all too easily become attached to, and apparently explained by, his Jewishness.

Renoir gambled that he and Dalio would be able to present a marquis whose charm and humanity would always make a larger impression than his corruption, a character who would amuse and beguile us with his accomplishments and whose weaknesses would make us see more, not less, of ourselves in him. It was a similar gamble to the one placed with *If Love has wings* … The movie describes a 'decaying little world of pretentious and corrupt bourgeois' – Dalio's words[36] – through a tale of adultery and amorous intrigue. So it risks a puritan reaction that takes loose sexual activity for the sign and the source of decadence. (According to such a reading, the community's acceptance of an openly homosexual character would be a mark of depravity rather than maturity.)

La Règle du jeu achieves a balance that depends crucially upon the warmth and wonder earned by Dalio's performance. As so often in the cinema, our feelings about the character go together with our responses to the actor. Admiration for the spectacle that Dalio presents, its amazing variety of moods and shading of motives, belongs in the same frame with the love and sympathy we can feel for Robert de La Chesnaye, stranded in a world that requires falsehood but defeats generosity.

4 Christine (Nora Gregor)

One must be light of heart and light of hand, to hold and take, hold and let go … Life punishes those that are not so. (The Marschallin, Act One, *Der Rosenkavalier*, 1911, Richard Strauss, Hugo von Hofmannsthal)

With Jurieu's arrival at the airport, *La Règle du jeu* sets out images of the modern, and prepares a contrast with resistances to modernity. Almost as quickly it introduces themes of friendship and sexual passion. Octave the friend is at Le Bourget to greet Jurieu with relief and a warm embrace; his feeling for André is unembarrassed, available to the public eye and independent of any concern for the flier's achievements. Then Jurieu's outburst against the 'disloyal' absentee shows the fury of a disappointed lover and the disruptive force of a romantic obsession.

Octave's efforts to calm his friend are heard on either side of an abrupt transition as the film cuts to the view from behind a wireless set, its valves and other workings exposed to us. The apparatus, we now find, squats within a luminous space where decoration is prized well above utility. The camera rises to reveal a luxuriously appointed bedroom and to give us a full-length view of a woman who stands immobilised as a maid works to arrange the train of her evening gown. Both women have their eyes on the radio, so are looking toward us, as the announcer makes excuses for the great aviator. Breaking out of her paralysis, the woman we shall shortly come to know as Christine walks forward and, after a few more pensive moments of listening, reaches to switch the broadcast off.

The continuity identifies this woman as the object of André's outburst. As she moves away from her maid, she addresses her as 'Lisette' and, speaking with a pronounced Austrian accent, she asks for her evening purse. Her words and her expression give little away even when, at the radio, we see her in close-up. The camera is placed to reveal everything that her face and gestures make available to view, but it is less easy to determine her reaction than to say what it is not. She is not in a rage, though she has heard more than she wants to hear. She is neither amused nor dismissive. While the broadcast events are evidently provoking unhappy reflection, we lack the context for a more precise understanding of her mood or the direction of her thought.

Other things, however, we can see clearly – and some of them are surprising. Christine is a woman of a certain age. She lives in an environment of wealth and the culture of luxury, pressed thereby to display sophisticated command of its resources. Yet she lacks style. She is tall and her movement is ungainly; she has the awkwardness of an adolescent boy who has outgrown his strength. Her dress (by Chanel) is an expensive, gauzy miscalculation – fussily decked out at the neckline and cut lower in the back than any well-wisher would

advise. It exposes her arms and shoulders without flattery. In the bow and flowers that bedeck her hair, as in her dress, Christine seems to cling to a girlishness unsuitable to her years. It is rapidly apparent that Lisette, in a dress of simple black with a white bow at its neck, carries herself and her clothes with more chic than her mistress. It is hard to see Christine as a woman who could flourish in Parisian high society, and we may need to recall that young, conventionally attractive women are not the only ones who inspire lust and longing.

Christine's movement away from Lisette briefly reveals a rug on the floor behind her: the pelt of a polar bear with its jaws agape. Within seconds of our introduction to the La Chesnayes' way of life, we may glimpse the first of the dead things and the imitations of life that fill out its decor. Warmth in the exchanges between mistress and servant is achieved despite the scale of the setting and the sharp brilliance of its lights, some of which show on screen in nearly every shot. Their presence is amplified by the surrounding mirrors that enlarge the space even while they turn it inwards. Drapes, art objects and tapestries are everywhere, and much more apparent than windows or any other opening onto the world beyond. The radio is out of place here, intrusive in its looks as well as in its function.

Renoir makes a direct cut back to the night scene at the airport just as Christine is about to stop Radio-Cité's invasion of her chamber. An engineer pours a bucketful of technical talk into the hole that the hero's outburst has left. Then, away from the microphone, Octave and André share rueful moments as they reflect on the gaffe, and wonder about its impact on Christine. By linking the airfield and the La Chesnayes' residence, Renoir asserts the relationship between Jurieu and Christine as a main concern of the drama. The continuity is that of the film, not of the characters: when Christine turns the radio off, Renoir repossesses the sound sequence by switching back to the broadcasters at the airfield. This bluntness insists on a variety of viewpoints that only the film can achieve.

The cut is inspired, because it makes us share the men's uncertainty. It establishes Christine as a woman whose thoughts and feelings we shall not easily fathom. Had the camera stayed with Christine and Lisette, anything they did or said, their silence, their movement or their stillness, would have read as responses to the radio drama. When we return to Christine, those too eloquent moments have passed. Events have moved on and Christine has found unproblematic – apparently unrelated – topics of conversation. The cut strengthens the contrast between the crowded dark outside and the space and light within. As there is no longer continuity of sound from the broadcast, silence in Christine's chamber displaces the airport's turmoil.

We are looking at an ornately mirrored dressing table and it is a while before Christine, then Lisette, enters the frame.[37] An unpeopled image displays the camera's indirect approach to the drama. Nothing is offered (for instance, by a close-up or an exchange of looks) as a reaction to what has recently been heard. While continuing with her toilette, Christine makes small talk with the maid, quizzing her on her marriage to Schumacher, for details of her love affairs, and for her thoughts on the possibility of friendship with a man. The scene is played mainly on Lisette, starting with her face reflected in the mirror, but when it comes to the matter of friendship, the pace changes and we go to Christine in a large and lovely close-up.

There is contradiction here. Christine's gestures suggest the weight of the issue. As she is leaving, she stops halfway across the room, turns back to face Lisette and takes a moment before speaking. 'And friendship? What do you make of that?' Her words sound casual but the pause suggests deliberation. Her tone of voice is playful, or it affects playfulness. Once again the move to close-up invites us to look for the truth within, while the action is staged in a way that withholds definition of the marquise's state of mind. Having shown André with his emotions unguarded to a fault, the film-maker has prepared contrasts that make us feel – even if we do not think about – the uncertainty of our access to Christine's thoughts and feelings. Christine has a confidante in Lisette as André has in Octave, but whereas André unburdens himself to his friend and to the world, Christine does the reverse. She enquires into her maid's personal life just when the film has made us ready for further insights into her own.

Lisette's untroubled frankness offsets the reserve of her mistress. After two years of marriage, it suits her that Schumacher's job at La Colinière keeps him from being bothersome. Her happiness is in her life with Christine. She is indulgent towards the flimsy carnality that you have to expect of men, and amused to be its target so long as she decides when and where to take her pleasure. In asking nothing better than absence of her husband, and in taking love easily (with, among others, Octave), she presents a life on which Christine is an inquisitive spectator.

What is Renoir up to? By contriving that our first sight of Christine shall also give us our first sight of her maid, he has favoured characterisation of Lisette, and of the servant–mistress relationship, over the presentation of Christine's marriage. He has

avoided the obvious path that the exposition might have taken.
Choosing to delay the introduction of Robert, he has refused a scene in
which the La Chesnayes, man and wife, would have been together to
hear André's accusation. While having Christine offer no comment on
Jurieu and no response that suggests her view of their relationship –
this despite the force of his claims on her – the director has arranged
things so that Christine's first conversation shows her raising questions
about marriage, and happiness in marriage, and in that context
wondering about the pursuit of physical as well as romantic love.

The unsettled mood of the scene depends on mixed registers.
Christine asks her questions in a tone of playful nosiness. But she
asks so many, in such rapid succession, as to create an air of
insistence at odds with the voice. As if needing more than the maid's
happy self-assurance, Christine presses further into detail: What do
your lovers say to you? Do they hold you? Take your hand?
Then what?

An atmosphere of banter and badinage is reasserted at intervals
by moves into unserious conflict, as when Lisette pretends to have
lost Madame's lipstick. But there is something effortful in Christine's
high spirits. Set against the briskness of Lisette, Christine's manner is
of a woman trying to combat a draining weariness. Certainly she is
calling on her maid for company and distraction, enlisting her
collusion in refusing to ascribe any significance to the radio's tidings.
Perhaps Jurieu's accusation has disturbed her more than she can
acknowledge. But it could be that she is threatened by a more general
lassitude, even despair.

Her movement is strange. She walks eyes down with a slight
stoop and a soldierly working of her arms. Her natural gait seems to
be a stride but as she heads for the door and out of her room, she
toils as if uphill or against a strong wind. She smiles at the right
moments but the smile does not stay on her face; her features relax
into nothing as strong as misery but something less than
contentment and much less than happiness. Her speech has a sighing
cadence; it reaches for brightness but does not sustain it. On the

question about friendship and in bidding Lisette goodnight, she hits a heartbreak note.

These are matters of tone, not of statement. A director can use close-ups of secret moments to vouchsafe insight into the true states of thought and feeling. Renoir avoids this rhetoric completely and grants Christine a peculiar privacy both in his use of the camera and in his construction of the drama. Through all the scenes of exposition, Christine faces not a single question about her relationship with, or feelings towards, Jurieu.

Consider the first words between husband and wife:

ROBERT   We're late, my darling.
CHRISTINE   As always.

A wife who is always late for social engagements is one who is at least not eager in her appetite for them. This scene, introducing Robert, follows on from the interrupted radio broadcast and Christine's boudoir conversation with Lisette. Had we been told that Christine was late and that her husband was waiting for her, we would have been pushed to notice her delaying and to wonder about it. But now when Robert remarks on lateness, we hear his words in their immediate context, which is the broadcast from Le Bourget. Robert is listening in his study. Noticing his wife's arrival, he first turns the radio off, as if embarrassed to have been caught eavesdropping. 'We're late' is his claim to have used the radio only to pass the time. The words are also his offer to ignore Jurieu's tantrum, even to pretend not to know that Christine is its unnamed subject. He is leaving Christine to decide whether and how to account for her involvement. Robert's first words show his aptitude for avoiding difficult issues, and for enabling others also to avoid them.

By lingering, Christine acknowledges that, late as they may be, the two of them cannot hurry on. She herself opens the Jurieu question but does it obliquely by claiming to like one of Robert's mechanical dolls, and the tune that it plays, better than the radio.

Given this tiny cue, Robert jumps in to make his wife's excuses for her. 'I can imagine what happened,' he says, introducing a fantasy of the liaison that he develops at some length. He spins a story in which the naive aviator, foozled by desire, has misjudged Christine's offers of friendship and support. His tone is whimsical; it displays that he can without qualm or anger – rather with an amusement that patronises Jurieu – put his imagination to work on intimate scenes from his wife's time with her suitor. There's no Othello in the making here.

In a whirl of joy and relief, Christine affirms the tactful tale. She does not suspect – nor do we – that her husband has spoken with more diplomacy than candour. We shall learn later, in passing, that his confidence in Christine's loyalty is less than solid. We shall find out too that all of society can put a name to the target of André's accusation. As the film develops, it will play intricate variations on the themes of belief and judgment – what people take for knowledge (in the realm of motive, feeling, intimate relationships) and what they do about their knowledge in the social world. We shall be shown repeatedly how context and viewpoint govern what people make of the things they see and hear. Renoir gives us an awareness that his characters mainly lack, of the uncertainty of judgment and the precarious bases of belief.

Christine entered the scene under an obligation to offer an account of or an apology for events at Le Bourget. We may or may not observe the oddity of Robert's taking on the job of explaining (away) events in which he himself had no role. As our first view of their marriage, the scene models the structure of their relationship, with Robert effusive and Christine largely silent. This is vital background to the scene in which Christine will herself have to take centre stage as hostess – with the assembled guests an alert audience – to welcome André to La Colinière. Her speech will derive many of its cues from Robert's inventions here. For the moment, we are most likely to take from the scene impressions of Robert's eagerness to please and of a good friendly marriage with room for playfulness and courtesy.

How differently the scene would play for us if we already knew what we shall shortly learn – about Robert's infidelity. Confident in our possession of the truth behind appearances, we would become superior spectators on Robert's performance of trust and Christine's avowal of her belief in him. The action of the scene would be explained in advance as an exposure of Robert's bad faith and his wife's blindness. Renoir arranges the drama so as to avoid narrowing the terms of our understanding. The surprises that he springs do not simply exchange one set of assumptions for another. Rather they produce a less and less easily defined complex of fact and possibility.

We are given a brilliant, spare and suggestive exposition, one that will be completed in the next scene as Robert fails to extricate himself from his affair with Geneviève. But its ease and clarity are in tension with its reticence over what it has set up as the main issue: Christine's feelings towards André Jurieu. Beyond the little drama of Robert's invention, we have only André's disappointment to indicate how matters stood before the airport outburst. By making Christine's excuses for her, Robert has deprived us of an opportunity to hear her side of the story. We shall never hear it.

Christine has opportunities to unburden herself not only to Robert but also to Octave, Lisette, André, even Geneviève. But when she speaks of Jurieu, it is only to retail her husband's narrative of a misunderstood kindliness. In what may be the film's most debated moments and in a scene ostensibly of revelation, Renoir creates a climax of withholding. It comes after the animal massacre, and with it forms a pair of turning points halfway through *La Règle du jeu*. The first is tonal: once subjected to the savagery of the slaughter, death has been put on our agenda and we cannot continue to take the film lightly, as comedy in the vein of Beaumarchais or indeed Lubitsch. The second turn is dramatic: Christine's discovery of her husband's adultery. Fear of this exposure has given Geneviève her hold over Robert. They agree in taking it for granted that Christine

could never forgive the deception practised on her in the three years of her marriage.

We are reminded of this assumption in the immediate prelude to the discovery. While Christine and Octave are in a group larking about and exploring the telescopic powers of a field lens, Robert and his mistress are walking elsewhere in the same boggy landscape. Yet again they are dissecting their relationship, one of whose main and morbid features – in marked contrast to that between husband and wife – is always to be under discussion. In a scene written and acted to perfection, Geneviève at last accepts the loss of Robert's love but wins from him a final nostalgic embrace. Renoir cuts back to Christine's group, where the general passes her the lens so that she may enjoy a glimpse of distant birdlife. She surveys the scene, smilingly resisting Octave's boisterous demand to have a look, but her smile disappears as she pauses to check a sight she has chanced upon. An insert gives us her view of

Christine's vision of infidelity

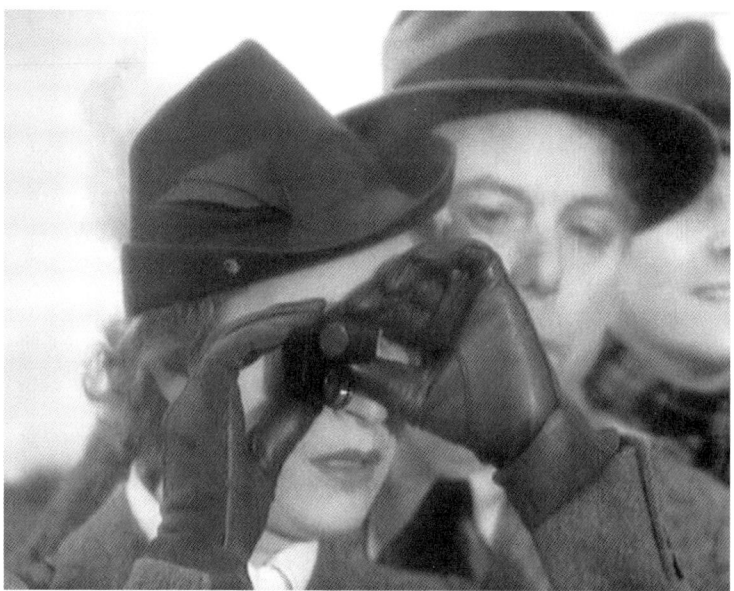

her husband and Geneviève in an embrace. Then a cut in to
close-up shows Christine fixed in contemplation of the sight.
Octave remarks that she seems to have discovered something
interesting. 'Very interesting,' she replies, and the tone of her voice
attracts Octave's concern. He is no longer playful. This image is
held as the sequence ends on a fade to black.

   That leaves us uninformed about Christine's reaction.
To continue the scene would inevitably mean giving us insights into
her response; she has, after all, to walk back to the chateau with her
guests and an inquisitive Octave. (Beyond that, she will predictably
have to encounter Robert and Geneviève over the supper table.)
Her 'Very interesting' has more poise than a stunned silence, but it
gives nothing away. As she maintains her hold on the field lens,
Christine's eyes are obscured by her black gloves, so her face is of one
in a mask. Only the soundtrack, bringing us the melancholy sound of
a distant horn, hazes the scene with a twilight sadness. At this point

'Something interesting?'

of shocked vision, Christine's image is in effect one of unseeing and, since she remains motionless, of straining to see.

A chapter has been closed. On a dying note from the horn, Renoir's fade to black declares finality. We could now expect an early display of the results – the immediate results – of Christine's discovery. Instead Renoir fades in on a morning scene; an evening and a night, at least, have passed. A clock is chiming. Marceau is in the corridor gathering up the guests' footwear. Christine is there too, in her dressing gown. (So she has not straightway left the chateau.) Her response to Marceau's respectful greeting is hesitant, indicates less than perfect composure. On the other hand, she is not manifestly discomposed. Nothing suggests how she has passed the time since returning from the marshes, what have been her thoughts and what she now intends. She is up early; has she slept? She walks towards a door, has a moment of doubt, but makes up her mind to knock. Marceau watches as she goes in. The smooth, conventional cut would cross to the interior on Christine's entry, but the camera stays with Marceau for some seconds – as if he needed watching as much as his mistress.

When the cut comes, we find Christine making friendly approaches to Geneviève, who is packing for departure and understandably wary (this is the first time she has been alone with her ex-lover's wife). Her tension offsets Christine's apparent ease, as her quick, jerky movements play against the stillness of her visitor, leaning relaxed against the door. Packing gives her a pretext for darting back and forth evading Christine's steady gaze, and under questions posed with such kindly concern that courtesy compels an answer. The wife has the initiative here. She may or may not know why she has sought this meeting, but Geneviève must wait and wonder.

Having discovered herself deceived, Christine now becomes a deceiver. Her 'frank talk' involves pretence that she has for a long time accepted both her husband's adultery and the public knowledge of it. She invents a Robert whose lies can always be seen through and whom she can reproach only for his habit of smoking in bed.

On these last points, she draws Geneviève into laughing collusion. Pressing her to stay for the fete, she claims to want Robert's attention diverted while she pursues an intrigue of her own. We cannot tell what truth or reason there might be in this.

The scene ends with a display of girlish high spirits, though Geneviève now has as much cause for bewilderment as Christine. She, with Robert, had supposed Christine to be ignorant of the affair. They know nothing of the spyglass's disclosure, and they have shared the belief that discovery would destroy the marriage. Moreover the wife has invited her to stay on as Robert's lover when Robert has most recently admitted to having lost interest in her. With no moment of thought about it, Geneviève has fallen into acceptance that she will remain at La Colinière. We are not invited to ask what she wants or what she expects.

Convention would have this scene followed by events that reveal both the reality of Christine's state of mind and the process

A frank conversation?

between Robert and Geneviève when, as surely she must, she tells him what she has just learned. Renoir gives us none of this. In a state of hilarity, Christine and Geneviève leave the bedroom as a pair to find turmoil in the corridor. Half the male guests are in an uproar over the non-return of their footwear. Among them is Octave, whose greeting both women receive amid the hubbub as if nothing unusual has happened. Christine takes charge as hostess, with care only for the comfort of her guests, and looks forward with everyone to the fun to be had at the festivities in honour of Jurieu.

The mask that Christine assumed out in the marshes remains in place. She may not quite know what she is doing but she is doing it with impressive poise. If she came to learn from Geneviève what she was unready to extract in a confrontation with her husband, then sharing a joke about Robert's messing the bedsheets with cigarette ash would be a clever way of confirming that the affair has gone on long enough to become routine. What else in her performance may be pretence we cannot be sure.[38]

La Règle du jeu places us as witnesses to the spinning of tales and the telling of lies. Here pretence has been made central to a scene of truth-seeking. In the lie that Robert cannot lie, Christine denies the reality of her disappointed trust and, in the semblance of frivolity with which it is offered, she puts herself in defiance of her deepest values. She is no longer in character, and she is a long way out of it when she goes on to lament the dullness of Jurieu's sincerity. Maybe she is striving to remodel herself in her image of Geneviève. She has not only elicited a collusion *entre femmes*. She has aligned herself with Geneviève's worldview by echoing her speech, affecting to find sincere people a ghastly bore, *assommant* – a word that sits naturally on Geneviève's tongue (we've heard her use it twice) but not on her own. The movement of the scene is from separation, through pursuit and evasion, to unity; the two leave the bedroom as a dancing pair in closely matched costume.

The note of hysteria in the women's high spirits is amplified by the riot in the corridor over the missing shoes. It's as if the derangement in Christine's psyche has let loose a general disorder. From this moment, there's a kind of mad-gas in the air. It will turn the Jurieu festival into a night of fools, where fancy dress may act as disguise or may force an exposure of truths more conveniently ignored. The density of Renoir's dramatic imagery shows in the use of Marceau – token of the marquis' effort to wish away barriers and choices – as the immediate cause of disarray. But the lightness of his touch may be seen as he affirms a shift in the film's register with a scene where chaos is merely absurd: the loss of shoes is an issue of no weight or consequence but the men protest as if calamity has engulfed their world.

Perhaps the mad-gas has been seeping into the film ever since the game-shoot. I mean into the film, not just its characters. The scene in the marshes, turning point of the plot, is quite odd. The little telescope acts less like a marvel of modern optics than an instrument of bad magic; it reveals to Christine a sight that is completely invisible to her companions looking in the same direction. Meanwhile, proposing this dank terrain as the setting for their *bel adieu*, Robert and Geneviève behave as if secure in the privacy of a very open space. And yet when Geneviève, while seeking a gesture of tenderness, recalls the time when there was no Christine to spoil things for her, she turns into camera. We see that she averts her eyes from Robert, from which we may understand that she prefers the lover she can conjure up in memory to the ex-lover who stands before her. The moment has that depth and sadness. Yet the turn – with a cut in to enlarge it – occurs right on the mention of Christine and leaves Geneviève gazing out across the marshes as if in bitterness and defiance, wishing upon Robert's wife the pain that is her own. The possibility of inflicting the wound of knowledge has been a constant theme. So the image suggests what the action denies, that Geneviève feels Christine's presence and is staging for her eyes a scene of betrayal.

Another oddity is Renoir's omission of the circular masking that is the standard signal of a telescopic viewpoint. Neither of the images through the spyglass, first of a squirrel then of the love-makers,

carries this mark – which Renoir had himself employed in *Boudu
sauvé des eaux*. Cutting, camera angles and squeezed perspective
leave us in no doubt what we are seeing. But where the vignette
ordinarily works to stress the remoteness of the object and the
subjectivity of the vision, Renoir avoids a format that would give
these images a status other and less than that of the surrounding
views. They are all products of his camera and he does not seek to
limit either their authority or his own responsibility for them.

The owner of the field lens (Berthelin) has boasted that it allows
examination of wildlife without scaring it off and with full entry into
its private life. What Christine sees, accurately, is Robert taking
Geneviève into his embrace. In its isolation, the image seems to reveal
her husband as the instigator of love-making with a Geneviève
responsive to his approach. Renoir offers just this one image and by
not cutting back for a further view ensures that we feel this moment
to be frozen into Christine's consciousness.

Matters of interpretation now face us both in our effort to see behind Christine's mask and in our perception of the reading she has made of the spyglass's information. Central to the effect is the simultaneous eloquence and opacity of the gestures we witness. We have learned a great deal but we cannot rely upon our understanding of what we have learned. By now, criticism of *La Règle du jeu* may have overstressed the irony of Christine's misreading the lens's perfected image, vital as that is. When she at last gets to speak about her disillusionment to Octave and Lisette, blaming them for keeping the truth from her for so long, her key thought is that the last three years of her life have been based on deception. Her past is sullied now that she reviews it with herself as dupe and target of the world's patronage. Knowing the affair to be over would not change that.

She says that seeing the pair together she 'suddenly understood'. But is the deception all that she has in mind? If so, she would not be confronting the sense of her life's hollowness that was

'I suddenly understood'

hers, half-recognised, even before the massacre of wildlife and illusions out in the marshes. Renoir showed us this in a touching scene where he most clearly shadowed Christine with the figure of the countess in Beaumarchais' – and even more Mozart's – *The Marriage of Figaro*. In a famous aria, 'Dove sono', Mozart gives the countess a heart-searching lament for the passing of time and youthful happiness. But where Mozart's countess is reacting to the knowledge of her husband's faithlessness, Renoir places Christine's 'aria' well before the revelation of Robert's affair.

The scene in question forms the latter part of a single take, more than a minute long, in which Renoir enlists the door to Christine's bedroom as an eloquent extra player. It comes at a point where, as far as she knows, the immediate problems have been resolved. She has, to general acclaim, performed the introduction of Jurieu as (no more than) a dear friend. Now, in contrast with a rumpus of noisy goodnights in which she is again on display as the perfect hostess, we see her struggle with the threat of a future defined by frustration and regret. Having finished with Lisette for the night and sent her away, Christine calls her back into her room as if fearful of solitude. When she asks if Lisette shares her desire for children, she cannot disguise her longing and her anxiety. She needs the claims that children would make upon her time and her attention. In articulating this need she exposes an emptiness and a conviction of present uselessness that her achievements in hospitality do nothing to assuage.

The dialogue's concern with time is doubled in the action, since summoning Lisette again, without a task to give her, is itself a call for help in occupying some threatening minutes. (It turns out that Lisette is too excited by the thought of dallying with Marceau to be able to share her mistress's worries for more than a few seconds.) The end of the scene is played across the line of the door as Lisette exits in evident eagerness to get back into the communal swim. After a teasing hint that Christine might treat herself to some fun with André Jurieu, Lisette pulls the door shut. Christine stands there, accepting solitude. Her closeness to despair, her fear of being left alone with her

thoughts, has no clear occasion. But when she needed someone to talk to, she chose her maid rather than her husband. It is with Lisette that she can speak about what matters to her, how she suffers and what she thinks would be the cure.

We have reason to wonder about this because Christine is holding her maid in conversation only moments after having said goodnight to her husband. The scene started as Robert freed himself from the attentions of his guests to seek out his wife. He made to follow her into her room but paused just across the threshold. Further progress was blocked by Christine as she turned at the door to face him. She listened to his effusive thanks and compliments, responding hardly at all. When he seized her hand in both of his and bowed to offer a kiss, both passionate and courteous, Christine bade him goodnight. These were words of dismissal, however warmly offered, and Robert understood that he had been sent away. He sought an opportunity for a more intimate exchange. Christine refused it. In closing the door, she shut Robert out where she could more easily have allowed him in. These moments were shaded with sadness, and the hint of finality, by the dying notes of a horn (playing the same mournful strain that will accompany her view through the field lens).

We know that Robert's love for his wife is embarrassed by his involvement with Geneviève. We know that he is in an unusual fix, burdened by the 'heavy cloak' of a lie and wishing to escape from the boredom of adultery into the excitement of marriage. That knowledge gives us – but does not dictate – a way of understanding why he struggles with his words and gestures in Christine's presence. We have no similar basis for an understanding of Christine. We may feel that the barrenness of her marriage has the force of metaphor but there must also be material reasons for it. The issue could have been clarified for us in a conversation between husband and wife. Instead we have been given the impression that Robert and Christine achieve only the avoidance of their most pressing concerns, and the avoidance is on Christine's side unaccounted for.

With Christine, Renoir takes to extremes his usual way with backstories and motivations – either to offer them bluntly or to withhold them altogether. There is no film author more concerned with character and less concerned with a psychology of origins, with how things and people came to be the way we find them. He bypasses explanation in favour of immediacy, seeking above all a vivid and infectious creation of mood. His characters present temperaments carried this way and that by the world's pressures. His work with the actors gives them a presence independent of the narrative moment. They betray themselves to the camera by their movements and postures, and by the way they speak more than by anything they say. The result is that understanding of their interior lives is reached sympathetically if at all: fellow feeling is our best guide to the shifting patterns of the life within.

We have seen Christine fighting off the knowledge of the falsity and frustration of her life. We have seen her struggling with a weariness that she could not name. If she is now starting to understand that she has deceived herself as much as she has been deceived, she is facing a larger problem than whether and how to repair her marriage. We might suppose this because clearly she has no idea what to do once she has left Geneviève's chamber. At the party she offers herself to a range of unsuitable, and in the case of Saint-Aubin unspeakable, partners. She wants to make off with André, then with Octave. She's drunk, of course, but it's the mad-gas that got her to drink too much.

At the end of the film, when death has sobered everyone, it's as if Christine has accepted the life of a puppet. Once more allowing Robert to take over the telling of her story, she re-enters the chateau prettily performing the role of the gracious hostess, but for how long no one could say. She has had – has apparently sought – no conversation with Robert since the shoot, though his courteous regard for her is maintained to the end. Discovering the corpse of Jurieu after the killing, she falls in a faint, which again withholds detail of her thought or feeling. (It could be that she faints with relief that the victim is Jurieu rather than the Octave for whom she has been waiting.) Once recovered she presents herself as an upholder of the proprieties, severely demanding self-control from a young admirer of André's as they head back from the murder scene: 'Jackie. People are watching you.' A film that started with a missile thrown at Christine's marriage has gone through much upheaval and one homicide to arrive at no resolution of her fate or desires.

Renoir proclaims the absence of resolution by having Christine collude with her husband in upholding appearances. Less markedly, the other main relationships are also up in the air. At the party, Geneviève has sniffed the mad-gas at least as deeply as her rival. Since we have been given no private moment between ex-mistress and husband, we have only Robert's exasperation to guide us when a shrieking Geneviève demands to know when he will take her away. It is equally disconcerting when, not much later, she calmly takes herself off to bed with a promise to see Robert in the morning. That's the last of her. Some of the incoherence in her behaviour may be attributed to Renoir's late decision to reinsert the character into the screenplay halfway through shooting, rather than have her leave before the celebration. It's hardly conceivable that the part would be written this way in a polished shooting script. But Mila Parély carries everything off with shrill gusto and complete conviction. She makes it easy to believe that her character was retained largely because the director was so enchanted with her performance.

Lisette has secured her main aim – to be kept in the service of Christine. But what of her marriage? We have had no clue about what could have induced her to yoke herself with Schumacher, a man to whom she is cruelly indifferent. But now she has had a demonstration of his murderous devotion: he was prepared to kill her alongside her partner in a weightless dalliance. We are better informed about her professional prospects than whether she cares to resolve the turmoil in her erotic life. Her marriage is a barren soil for the tenderness and fellow feeling she has shown in loving farewells to both her recent suitors. Snatching a little time from her obligations to

Christine, she has assured Marceau and Octave of her affection with
no thought that they can be together again. This shift of moods
suggests depth beyond Lisette's charming appetite and brightness.
In her closing moments, Paulette Dubost defines with finesse the
mingling of whim with concern.

In all these cases, Renoir avoids resolution by conducting
matters so that there are no occasions for private talk between the
principal pairs. Solicitous for Christine at the door of the chateau,
Robert bows low to kiss her hand and seems to assume that they will
be leaving together in the morning. Christine has not responded to
Robert's attentiveness – putting his hand on her shoulder, adjusting
the hang of her borrowed cloak – and before she was called back by
his words she seemed to have found a cause for hurrying straight
inside. Pulled back into the public gaze, she offers no more than a
polite 'Goodnight, Robert'. After the briefest meeting of their eyes,
Christine lifts her head to scan the onlookers, takes a breath and

manages a gracious smile to bid them goodnight. Christine has
class, and the smile must correspond to her sense of what's proper.
It has required effort but it says nothing else about her feelings.
Then La Chesnaye's public explanation displaces any private
settlements. Almost the whole weight of the finale is carried by
Robert, by Marcel Dalio.

Throughout the film, in fact, Renoir tends to bounce Nora
Gregor's scenes off other actors. It is well known that he became
afraid early in the filming that he had made a mistake in casting her.
Twenty years later, working on *The Golden Coach*, he was still
recalling that 'Nora Gregor's awkwardness came close to killing that
film'.[39] She was an experienced actress on stage and screen, in
Hollywood as well as in Vienna. But the role had not been conceived
for an Austrian and she did not speak French. Renoir made
adjustments, but it is clear that he insisted on having the character
fluent and refined in her use of French, with no *Wie sagt man das?* to

excuse fumbles and hesitations. That may be one source of the strain that shows in the performance and that shows the more against the ease and precision of Dalio, Dubost, Parély. They demonstrate a wit and a lightness of touch that is not in Nora Gregor's range.

It must have been disconcerting for Renoir to find his 'Marianne' lacking in caprice, and struggling to unite emotional depth with finesse. Evidently he judged that strong action was needed to bring out Gregor's most affecting qualities – her eagerness, hunger, confusion – while compensating a heaviness more appropriate to melodrama than to a dramatic fantasy. The determination is most apparent in Christine's big scene – her speech to the guests at La Colinière explaining her friendship with Jurieu. Here Renoir holds her only briefly in close-up before putting himself and Dalio centre frame in the background performing antics that draw visual attention away from Christine while her words keep the monopoly of the soundtrack.

This outrageous upstaging must have challenged the player's forbearance and suggests the scale of Renoir's unease. But we should thank Renoir's luck for the awkwardness of Nora Gregor. He could certainly have obtained a lighter, more capricious Christine from his first choice, Simone Simon. But that would have smoothed the tone whose unevenness is so vital to the film's originality. With a more comfortable performance from its leading lady, *La Règle du jeu* would not be the masterpiece we have today.

It is our gain that Christine has more variety than consistency. At her rare moments of relaxation, she is enchanting, a lovely playmate. At her wariest, we feel the frailty of her defences. The strange meeting of the stolid and the delicate that we see in Nora Gregor gives her a gauche quality that sits in tension with her practised etiquette. On-screen characters remark on Christine as a foreigner, unaccustomed to Parisian ways. It is left to us to see the shyness that is only masked by her education in social performance. Nobody tells us what we can also see, that she is a brave and desperate woman, completely lost.

5 Octave (Jean Renoir)

Pirandello ... opened a new window on the infinite horizons of the collective imagination, and, like so many others, I certainly breathed some of that air.[40]

What goes for Christine and Nora Gregor goes also for the film. The flaws are evident, but so much a part of its character as to be aspects of its charm and of its achievement. It dances on a volcano, needing to fail in order to succeed. It denies itself a safe space of, say, ordinary effectiveness. If not heart-rending and funny, unique and profound, it must seem lurchingly eccentric with few points of rest between pretension and triviality, uninvolving as melodrama and elsewhere too strenuous for easy laughter. There are wonders of technique, and passages whose wit and delicacy would be hard to miss, but they come in collision with baldly contrived moments that could be taken for blunders if they were not – being readily avoidable – so clearly meant. Several such moments involve the figure of Octave, the part played by Jean Renoir himself.

Putting himself into a role so large and pivotal was the riskiest of all Renoir's gambles with casting. He had appeared in small parts in a number of films, most recently in his own *La Bête humaine*, where his amateurism was perhaps appealing, certainly clear. While his was a familiar image for the French public, he did not command the skills of a trained actor. Renoir includes in *La Règle du jeu* lapses of performance for Octave which, with any other actor, would surely have claimed the kindness of further rehearsal and another take. The timing stutters, so that we sense the actor recalling his next line or his next move.

If we see this, it must have been apparent to Renoir. His eye for performance is well attested by his collaborators as well as by his movies. In *My Life and My Films*, Renoir quotes with satisfaction an

agent's remark that he 'could make a wardrobe act'.[41] The spectacle
he provides as Octave is the spectacle he, the author, wanted. A clue
is given by another passage in the book that discusses Pierre
Champagne, a friend who appears in all his earliest movies.
The passage captures Renoir's stubborn obedience to his own taste,
his own sense of the camera's play with the beings it captures:

People were astonished by my persistence in using Pierre as a performer. …
One had to take or leave Pierre as he was. Such as he was, he invested the
parts he played with an unanswerable authenticity … He did not 'act' …
He was always Pierre Champagne, and this inability to change himself
obviously worked to the detriment of the plot … I did not let this trouble me.[42]

For most movie-makers, indifference to values detrimental to
the plot would be absurd. Renoir boasts of it with an awareness of
perversity relevant to his own case. His Octave was giving trouble
even while the film was in production. The business partners were
dismayed by what they saw in the rushes and complained that his
playing was no good. Renoir faced them down. Then, in the editing,
with anxiety growing about the film's reception, he was persuaded to
concentrate the cuts on scenes involving his own character.
And again, in reaction to the failed premiere, 'I cut the scenes in which
I myself played too large a part, as though I were ashamed, after this
rebuff, of showing myself on the screen.'[43] The viewers who were best
disposed, it seems, were his professional colleagues. Mila Parély,
interviewed in 1995,[44] and Paulette Dubost, in her 1992 memoirs, are
both full of praise; the failure they lament is of audiences insensitive to
Renoir's unanswerable authenticity. Dubost: 'In the role of Octave he
is sublime! Of course, Octave is him. He is marvellously natural …
Jean, so uneasy, feigning gruffness, so tender …'[45]

On the eve of the movie's premiere, Renoir told journalists that
he had wanted 'to be more inside the film … And for a part as special
as that of Octave – the confidant of all the others, the hero in spite of
himself – I could not see who else could play the part more

submissively.'[46] In another interview, he claimed to have recognised
that the character as he had written it 'corresponded to me almost
exactly, both physically and morally'.[47]

Pirandello's influence shows in the confusion that Renoir
promoted between Octave and the film's author. Casting himself in
the fictional role furthers the confusion but does not create it.
Many of the crossovers would still be in place with another actor in
the part. We are at key points shown how Octave helps the action
along. We see him propel André over the threshold as they arrive at La
Colinière. He is closely involved in Christine's discovery through the
spyglass. In the denouement, André is sent to his death by Octave, and
he dies in Octave's place: that's who Schumacher believes he has in his
gun sights. Moreover the gamekeeper believes he is killing a man
exposed in adultery with Lisette: one of the first things we learned
about Lisette was that Octave is one of her lovers. Octave dresses both
Christine and André for the fatal accident: he hides Christine's head

beneath the hood of Lisette's cloak, and he hoists his own overcoat onto André's shoulders as he sends him out for the fatal rendezvous.

The plot offers these actions as mischance. But there is one scene where Octave's intervention is blatant. On the first night at the chateau, in the sequence immediately before the hunt, he finds André in their bedroom dejected and of a mind to pull out. What could be better? Octave has done his bit, and André is giving up the chase. But here is Octave's reaction (accompanied by a suite of wanton gestures): 'Oh, no, chum! I went to enough trouble to get you here. Now that you are here, okay, here you stay.'

This is your author speaking! A gun shown in the first act has to be kept on hand and fired in the last. The fact is that Octave works harder at promoting a romance than André ever does at pursuing it. Where Octave keeps helping the affair along, poor André is at a loss when Christine's availability at last turns his fantasy of love into a real prospect. The realist in Octave could recognise that romantic

'Here you stay'

obsessions dissipate and that a dreamer can sooner or later tire of his dream. As a friend, he could be happy to see the waning of a morbid passion. But a storyteller cannot accept anything so hostile to form and drama. Renoir needs, and Octave is his means to supply, a climax. Octave had to fail as friend and go-between so that he could serve Renoir's goals as an author.

In casting himself as Octave and insisting on failure, Renoir let it be seen that he did not absolve himself from his film's critique. He did not supply himself with a mask but took the risk of self-exposure. In fancy dress, he wears a disguise that fits him so well it proves difficult to shed. He joins in the fete dressed as a bear – a big brown bear cruelly tamed to dance. He inhabits a shambling image of affability, danger, limited understanding and clumsiness.

Choosing this image as a trap for Octave, Renoir was choosing it for himself and choosing it in all its contradictory aspects. Clumsiness, for instance, was an accusation that Renoir was used to seeing pointed at his directing style. Jarring cuts occur in plenty, and

the relationship between action and image is often disconcerting – empty frames, lopsided compositions, a camera obstinately fixed to lose sight of the actors, or wandering as if in hope of chancing upon useful matter rather than advancing towards a revelation foreseen from the start.

In his much-interviewed later years, Renoir often declared his lack of interest in good carpentry, work that is well made in the sense that its finish disguises its construction. Renoir lets the joints show and often he has them obtrude. Some of his images are bluntly rhetorical, others – particularly in close-up – are emphatically composed, with the stillness of portraiture. His style embraces mismatch and refuses consistency. It particularly refuses a consistent negotiation between realism and displayed artifice. So in its prologue and at its end, *La Règle du jeu* models a polished formality at odds with the untidy happenstance that asserts itself elsewhere. For Renoir, alone among the great directors, elegance is not a standing ambition but a special effect, brought into play when it can aid expression. Whether in performance or in the structure of the image, elegance carries the sense of affectation, of a surface that serves to conceal unacceptable facts or feelings.

Renoir's cutting can be smooth, is often jolting, and it draws value from each of these tones. Though he must have been an editor's nightmare, he is celebrated for his skill in creating fluid group shots that respond to the mobility of the actors and create a deep, apparently unbounded space. There are long passages where movement flows within and between shots and where the sound is delicately engineered to hold everything together. The fete at La Colinière is renowned for such scenes, which Lourié's sets were designed to support. An instance among many occurs at the height of the chaos when all the main characters are engaged in pursuits or evasions, or both simultaneously. The camera follows Robert in his move from the corridor where he has been recruited by Marceau to assist his escape from Schumacher, who is attempting to hold on to his wife as well as to trap the poacher. Having spotted Schumacher entering from the outside with Lisette in tow, Robert stages a diversion in the foyer.

The cut positions the camera to look across the foyer so that the main staircase stands in the background with closed doors on either side: on its right, a few steps indicate the way down to the servants' quarters, while on the left nearest the main entrance stand the imposing double doors to a spacious gun room. Robert crosses the hall and calls to the gamekeeper, drawing him away from Marceau's place of concealment and causing him to release Lisette from his grip. With La Chesnaye and Schumacher in the foreground on either side of the frame, we have a clear view of Marceau's escape down to the kitchen and can observe Lisette as she begins to creep back in the same direction. Robert is still spinning out his orders when Berthelin approaches from behind the camera to interrupt him with a summons to return to the stage. As they leave, crossing the frame at the right foreground, Jurieu rushes in from the same direction to grasp Schumacher and demand help in finding Christine. Seeing her husband distracted, Lisette makes a break for the door downstairs. The noise of its closing signals her escape to Schumacher, who reacts by running back to fling open the door nearest to hand, that to the gun room. His action reveals Christine and Saint-Aubin within, and André rushes to confront them, pushing aside the gamekeeper, who then collides with Jackie, just arrived in search of André.

All this is observed by a camera fixed in position but scanning the scene to follow the movement of the figures. The group shot seems determined by a desire to encompass all the action and not to isolate particular elements or characters from the developing chaos, allowing us to see, for example, that Robert, while he concentrates on holding Schumacher's attention, still finds a moment to glance away and check on Marceau's escape. But the desired inclusiveness is defeated by the instability of the groups. We are not in the theatre, so space cannot hold the action. It spills out of the frame forwards, sideways and backwards. The music of an off-screen piano, even while it assists continuity, also maintains the presence of yet more action going on in other spaces.

When Jurieu barges into the gun room, the drama of his
challenge to Christine and Saint-Aubin is only one of the immediate
lines of continuity from the scene in the hall. Robert (who has urgent
unfinished business with Christine and Geneviève) has nevertheless
gone off all excited that the great moment has arrived to unveil his
limonaire. And Schumacher is furiously intent on recapturing his
errant wife (who has only seconds ago bunked off to be with
Marceau). Renoir has contrived three crises of equal weight and
obliged himself to choose which of them to follow. The actions point
in various directions and can no longer be offered in different sectors
of a single frame – not even in frames so crowded and so deep with
event as these have become.[48]

The camera could stay with Schumacher and let us see if he
now thinks to search the kitchen (and see what he may find there).
Instead we have a cut into the gun room to follow André's action,
but not directly. First there is a diversion away to the right, losing
André, to see Schumacher entangled with Jackie. Having passed up
the easy cut on André's approach to Saint-Aubin, Renoir comes
back to the same matter a few moments later, but now with a bump.
The clumsiness here is the forfeit paid for not wanting to lose track
of Schumacher. The jolt articulates nothing about the characters or
the action. But a bump is a blemish only if smooth continuity is a
prime value.

So it is, in most scenes in most movies. A bumpy cut calls for
an adjustment from the spectator that – to no useful effect – chops
against attention to developments in the world of the film. A great
deal of cutting-room craft goes into the achievement of the
undisturbed line. Fluency is hard to attain, and its product is a
sense, often a delightful sense, of ease. Skill makes labour disappear.
But Renoir's refusal of smooth continuity puts on screen, and makes
us feel, the difficulty of the choice between simultaneous and
competing lines of action. On what authority can André's crisis,
and Christine's, be given priority over Schumacher's or Marceau's,
even Jackie's?

The true oddity is that Renoir, so keenly suffering the agonies
of choice, should have fallen upon the movies as his medium.
The film-maker, more than any other artist, is in thrall to viewpoint.
Cameras and microphones are instruments of selection. What they
bring us is brought to the exclusion of everything else. The camera
demands placement; each image declares its angle of vision.
The availability of the cut means that the decisive moment occurs
once every fraction of a second. Renoir uses deep focus and the
scanning camera to strive against this condition, so presenting a
peculiar awareness of it. A movie-maker, not a painter manqué,
Renoir arranges the pattern of the shot rather than of the frame.
Unbalanced composition makes the world refuse to sit too neatly,
with seeming ease, within the format imposed upon it. The very
partial understanding that the spyglass affords Christine is a warning
against the limited vision that is the condition of a lens's revelations.

In the screenplay Renoir constructed a drama with many
separate but interacting crises. As *metteur en scène* he staged the
action to run across spaces never securely isolated from each other.
By these means he created conflicting lines of continuity as a manifest
problem for his camera. It seems to want to present an egalitarian, a
merely human, view of the action but its director cannot escape the
obligations of mastery, or authorship. In a medium that insists on
choice frame by frame, the style of *La Règle du jeu* collides the attempt
to keep everything in view against the impossibility of doing so.

So Renoir opts for clumsiness, inhabits the bearskin and shows
himself struggling against it. Octave's character takes these themes
into the drama. He wants an easy world. His generosity of feeling
makes him a good sort who hopes – perhaps also a coward who
pretends – to reconcile conflicting attitudes and interests. He takes it
on himself to rid his world of anguish and make it smile. Faced with
an insoluble problem and the pain it causes, he reacts – 'Leave it to
me. I'll sort it out' – and undertakes to help one friend seduce the
wife of another. But he is cast into gloom when reminded of the pain
that any success of André's would mean for Robert. Then he wishes

he could 'vanish down a hole … and not have to have my eyes open – not have to keep trying to sort out what's good, what's bad'. Ignoring what he knows, he persists in trying to organise the happiness of gamekeepers and poachers alike.

Or you could say that he doesn't want rabbits and doesn't want fences. He's in competition with La Chesnaye for the role of *meneur de jeu*. The difference is that La Chesnaye's concern is more with how things look than with how they are. And the marquis is unhappily aware of his own position inside the world that he's trying to control, while Octave is an arranger who sees himself as on the outside, a conductor – or a director – rather than a player.

That self-image involves a denial that he has interests on his own account. It contradicts what Renoir's presence on screen lets us see – that the director is also a player. The Pirandellian aspect of this is brought to climax in scenes between Octave and Christine, soft and slow scenes outside the chateau that offer brief release from the hysteria within. They begin with Octave on the terrace fantasising himself as Christine's father, a conductor of genius gifting his world with music and serenely accepting its thanks. In these scenes Renoir is a perfect actor, with telling gestures that take us inside the flow of Octave's mood. Alone at the imagined podium, he lifts his baton arm to release the first great chords, in counterpoint with wistful strains from a salon piano wafting out on the night air. But with the mismatch of that flimsy little waltz and the world-redeeming anthem evoked by memory and dream, Octave's arms slump to his side. The vision of the concert hall departs, the moment of triumph is lost, and he sinks to the ground to bump against the dank reality of hard stone steps. These are the same steps that will form the stage for La Chesnaye's final performance, when he offsets calamity with the reassurance of a world secured from challenge and change.

Though Renoir can seem to be forcing matters when delivering the ebullient Octave, loaded with exposition, free with explanation and opinion, he is always real and affecting in Octave's moments of let-down when he falls under the shadow of Chekhov's Uncle Vanya.

Octave's dream of artistry ... and its collapse

All Octave's bonhomie is an effortful flight from self-disgust.
At La Colinière, his manoeuvres to make things right for everybody
prepare the way for misery and slaughter. Inhaling the mad-gas
himself, he makes a brief, incompetent entry into the game of love
and must at last quit the scene and leave the stage to Robert's tidier,
more effective management.

If Octave knows himself for a failure, Renoir's film displays
itself as a failure of a different, related kind – in its inability to
sustain the mode of comedy where the author shows goodwill
towards the characters and the audience by ensuring that all may
come out harmlessly in the end. One way it earns this failure is by
giving death, and half-life, such a large and weighty presence.
Near the mid-point of the movie, when all the elements of high
comedy have been assembled, we are submitted to several minutes
of ugly carnage. Nothing in Renoir's story committed him to a hunt
scene, or required him to depict its process at length and in
displeasing detail. It is notable, too, that the sequence was retained
whole through all the cutting that tried to make the film more
palatable to the French public.

In his autobiography, Renoir writes of his detestation for the
cruelty of the hunt. Yet many animals were harmed in the making of
this film. Octave is present but a bystander. He carries no gun,
employs his hands in whittling a stick. If he puts himself outside the
sport, however, he makes no gesture of protest, or even of distaste;
and nothing but his own gregariousness compelled him to join the
party. He is off screen throughout the killing; to show him
uninvolved while the montage counts the victims of Robert,
Geneviève, Saint-Aubin, the general and others would define him too
clearly as an abstainer. Putting himself in and apart from the society
of the hunters, Renoir acknowledges the falsity of his position.

As the author of the film, Renoir was the author of the hunt
and of all the butchery needed to create its images of blood-letting
sport. He brought the reality of death into the centre of the fiction, in
a scene that remembers the slaughter of 1914–18 with fear for

slaughters to come. Organising his story round this event, he made it impossible for the film to cast off the shadow of massacre and reclaim lightness of heart. He was disingenuous in his claim not to have understood that audiences might find the movie upsetting. He ends the sequence by holding on the image of a rabbit, its flight halted by a bullet, its death throes piteously extended. It feels like a close-up and the seconds feel very long. With such images, which must be witnessed with pain and disgust, Renoir imposes a gulf between the attitudes of his characters and the feelings he elicits from us.

The dying rabbit is not the object of any character's interest or attention, but it is placed before us as the ultimate definition of the event we have been shown. Real animals die real deaths but are placed in a fictional world on screen. There they serve as objects, metaphors, markers of themes. In their victimhood they offer a more extreme reflection than any human actor of the camera's work in seizing the life of the world and turning it over as material for an artist (or an industry) to work with. How many rabbits had to be released into the path of waiting cameras and waiting guns to supply the perfectly articulated image of death agony with which to complete the sequence?

This little creature's end is contrived to serve the purposes of Renoir's rhetoric by finishing the massacre on a note of pathos. Through the placement of the image and through the extension of its time on screen, matched to the horn-call that ends the fun for everyone, the film-maker implicates himself in the sorrow he causes, recognising the price of eloquence, recognising the maker of this movie as the director of this killing.

There is another sense in which this death fulfils Renoir's design. It places the dead animal as a match to one we saw earlier. No sooner had Marceau on his first appearance seized with pleasure on his snare's small bounty than a rabbit that could have supplied his supper became instead the token of Schumacher's wardship over the rights of property. The stiffened corpse changed before our eyes from

a promise of nourishment secured by trespass, craft and labour into the dead symbol of law and social economy. (It is explicit, by contrast, that nobody wants to eat the beasts that have been flushed out as targets for the shooters, and as manifests of La Chesnaye's wealth and hospitality.)

Following the hunt, and following Christine's spyglass vision, Renoir pursues a double game. He carries the comedy into farce, as

'You want my rabbit?'

Schumacher is ever more outrageously provoked, but he develops also – to a startling degree – the imagery of the theatrical and of the deathly. First he puts all of the principals, and himself as the dancing bear, on stage to parade their patriotism with a chorus at once trivial and militaristic. (Conformity with its nationalist sentiment is asserted in the performance and affirmed in its reception.) Then he mingles performers and audience to create confusion about what is and is not a part of the show – about what is and is not, then, harmless. Next he gives us the Dance of Death.

Looking back on the film's production from the perspective of 1966, Renoir recalled how powerfully he had felt the meaning of the characters, the meaning of the action and 'above all the film's symbolic side'.[49] The *danse macabre* is saved from the banality or bombast of paraded symbolism by Renoir's love of the unpolished. It was a stroke of genius to conceive the entertainment that would contrast the love-chases not as a strictly formalised performance – of, say, a string quartet – but as a set of amateur theatricals, a show got up at short notice by a disparate group untrained in performing skills (and indulged by spectators who know they could not do better).

The dance is introduced by a weird effect, outrageous really, that lets us know that the mad-gas is everywhere, in the chateau and in the film. We have seen Berthelin backstage getting into a skeleton costume and too anxious about his performance to lend a hand in the real dramas that surround him. Ominous piano chords strike up, and this spooky music is complemented by a shrill of wind that brings the air of the graveyard to our ears. Then comes a close-up of piano keys, playing by themselves, as their tune becomes recognisably the start of Saint-Saëns' playful guignol. We know about player-pianos, but no mechanism is seen and the effect is magicked into the uncanny by the faces of bewildered onlookers as the camera drifts up and around towards the stage.

The trio of ghost figures up there present an amazing mix of the rough and ready with the inspired. They are costumed in bedsheets, with black eye sockets. Their dance is crudely prepared, with an air

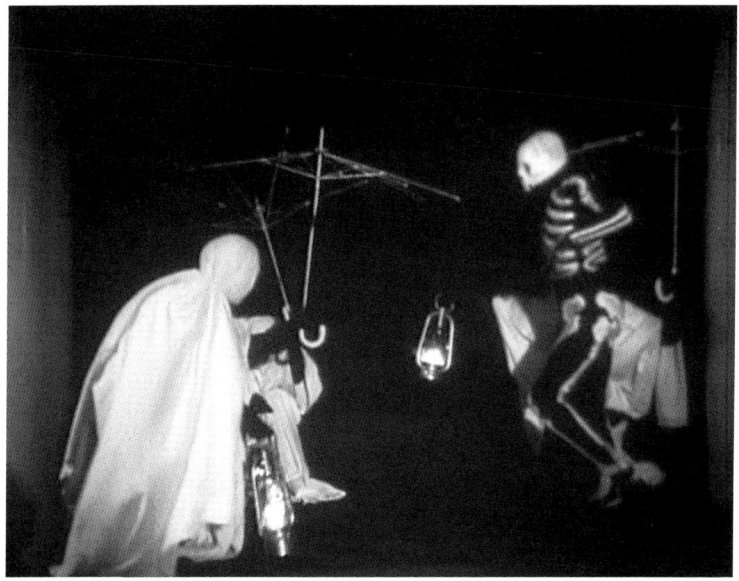

of what-do-we-do-next? But the skeleton theme from Berthelin's figure of death is brilliantly extended as each of them holds aloft the bones of a ruined umbrella. These comic emblems of mortality are what we see first when another makeshift produces the figures out of darkness head first: a black curtain winds down in front of them so as to picture their midnight surfacing out of the tomb. (Disney's *Skeleton Dance* of 1929 is in the background here.) Before running down from the stage to spread mock terror among the audience, they take up paraffin lamps, like dead men's censers, whose swinging gives a pretext for erratic light to madden the image. This lighting submits the off-stage world to on-stage effects and brings a sense of wildness, even intoxication, to the camera's attempt to keep up with the intrigues around Christine and Lisette.

The sound of the *Danse macabre* haunts the action as searches and pursuits collide. As long as we are in the chateau, music from the stage underscores all we see. From now on everyone is caught up in a show that has escaped control – Christine calls it *ce théâtre*, Robert wants an end to *cette comédie*. When finally the chaos finds its victim, there is distress but hardly any sign of surprise. In their first conversation, Robert identified Octave as a 'dangerous poet'. Now that their combined efforts at stage management have reached a deadly outcome, each of them has his own ending. The contrasts are marked. Octave's comes first, in a scene of farewells that begins on the terrace and leads away from the chateau. Receiving his goodbyes, Lisette understands that he is leaving for good. He sets out on foot along with Marceau, who was as much Robert's project as André was Octave's. Behind their conversation lies the knowledge that the poacher had become the gamekeeper's accomplice in an assault intended for Octave. This last goodbye is also the first time they have talked, but its tone is of the reluctant parting of old friends concerned for one another and united in remorse. (It could well evoke the au revoirs of the director and a favourite actor.) It ends with handshakes, saddened smiles and a

Farewell to Marceau

thought that, in an uncertain future for both of them, they just might meet again some day.

The start of a sorrowful exile is implied throughout the scene not in its psychology or through dramatic logic but in its atmosphere and imagery. Octave blames no one but himself. His mood seems to be of remorse rather than disgust, but he removes himself knowing that he no longer has a life within the La Chesnaye circle. In the background, bustle at the doors of the chateau contrasts with the uncertainty of Octave's movements. As he makes to leave, the camera pulls back, giving greater weight to the presence of the chateau and increasing the space that Octave must cross to quit the frame.

The imagery of dispersal that marks this scene is reversed in the last. All movement now is towards and into the chateau, and it is given the air of ceremony by the backing of the graceful, courtly music of Monsigny. But this elegance is also the triumph of theatricality over truth and the completion of tonight's dance of death. Symmetry is asserted. The aspect of a stage returns to the terrace from which Robert delivers his lies and his eulogy. After the principals have made their exits, their parade unblemished by the presence of a corpse, the aged general has his last word: he commends Robert's *savoir faire*, while lamenting it as the relic of a better past. Now the camera holds on a façade across which shadow after shadow passes into La Colinière. The cock has crowed, these dear ghosts give up their half-lives and, dignity intact, submit to the claims of the tomb.

Emphatic closure here displaces the loose, untidy movements of Octave's departure. Renoir's style, refusing neatness, embodies both a temperament and an ethical preference. It favours the loose and open values of friendship, generosity and hospitality over the stricter, more exacting concerns of obligation, rectitude and the law. The longing is for a human community where understanding and goodwill would collapse barriers and dissolve conflicts of interest. But if the poacher's interests and the gamekeeper's are both insisted upon, they cannot be reconciled. Nor can a wife's genial whimsicality survive a husband's

enforcement of exclusive rights in his sexual property. Octave and Robert have been at fault in ignoring the potential for violence in the variousness of needs and desires – their own as well as other people's. Everything shows that Renoir shares the wish to accommodate rather than discriminate. But in a world where the demand is to take sides, and where violence is approved, the lighter, looser values are under attack. To go into battle on their behalf is to set them aside and accept their defeat. With Schumacher justified and Octave in retreat, Renoir had already declared himself an exile from his society, and acknowledged his failure within it, before the catastrophes that one after the other befell his movie and his nation.

The general's verdict

Notes

1 Jacques Rivette and François Truffaut, 'Renoir Interview', *Cahiers du cinéma*, April 1954, in Carol Volk (trans.), *Renoir on Renoir* (Cambridge: Cambridge University Press, 1989), p. 6.

2 Jean Renoir, *Ma vie et mes films* (Paris: Flammarion, 1974), p. 157.

3 Claude Gauteur, *D'un Renoir l'autre* (Paris: Le Temps des Cerises, 2005), pp. 138–9.

4 Ibid., p. 145.

5 Renoir, *Ma vie*, p. 157.

6 Quoted by Jean Gaborit, discussing the film's reconstruction, on *The Rules of the Game* DVD, disc 2, Criterion Collection No. 216 (2004).

7 Marcel Dalio (with Jean-Pierre de Lucovich), *Mes années folles* (Paris: Éditions Jean-Claude Lattès, 1976), p. 133.

8 Paulette Dubost, *C'est court, la vie* (Paris: Flammarion, 1992), p. 100.

9 Eugene Lourie, *My Work in Films* (New York: Harcourt Brace Jovanovich, 1985), p. 70.

10 Henri Cartier-Bresson, 'A Memoir', in Lorraine LoBianco and David Thompson (eds), *Jean Renoir Letters* (London: Faber and Faber, 1994), p. 559.

11 Richard Roud, 'Memories of Resnais', *Sight & Sound*, Summer 1969, p. 127.

12 LoBianco and Thompson (eds), *Jean Renoir Letters*, p. 496.

13 Ibid., p. 393.

14 Penelope Houston, 'Venice Festival Report', *Sight & Sound*, Summer/Autumn 1969, p. 143.

15 Interview in *Pour Vous*, 28 June 1939, reprinted in Bernard Chardère (ed.), *Premier Plan*, Nos. 22–4, May 1962, p. 276.

16 Quoted in LoBianco and Thompson (eds), *Jean Renoir Letters*, p. 59. Note that Renoir expected a 'next time'.

17 Quoted in John McGrath and Maureen Teitelbaum (trans.), *The Rules of the Game* (London: Lorrimer Publishing, 1970), p. 13.

18 Quoted in Christopher Faulkner, *Jean Renoir: A Guide to References and Resources* (Boston, MA: G. K. Hall & Co., 1979), p. 124.

19 Volk (trans.), *Renoir on Renoir*, p. 237.

20 Jean Renoir, 'On me demande ...', *Cahiers du cinéma*, January 1952, p. 8.

21 Jean Renoir, *My Life and My Films*, trans. Norman Denny (London: Collins, 1974), p. 170.

22 Volk (trans.), *Renoir on Renoir*, p. 203. *Tanz auf dem Vulkan* was the title of a German movie from 1938 set in the Paris of 1830.

23 From an interview with Renoir in June 1966, for the television programme directed by Jacques Rivette in the series *Cineastes de notre temps*. Transcribed in Jean Narboni (ed.), *Jean Renoir: entretiens et propos* (France: Petit bibliothèque des Cahiers du cinéma, 2005; first published 1979), p. 281.

24 Olivier Curchod (ed.), *La Règle du jeu: nouveau découpage integrale* (Paris: Le Livre de Poche, 1999), p. 37.

25 Roland Toutain, *Mes quatre cents coups* (Paris: Amiot Dumont, 1951), p. 96.

26 McGrath and Teitelbaum, *Rules of the Game*, p. 13.

27 In *Les Caprices de Marianne*, it is Octavio who has the last word.

28 He addresses the gamekeeper as 'vous' but the poacher is straightway a 'tu'.

29 Seen also in *La Grande Illusion*, *La Marseillaise* and *La Bête humaine*. See Renoir's 1966 tribute to Carette in Claude Gauteur (ed.), *Jean Renoir: Ecrits (1926–1971)* (Paris: Pierre Belfond, 1974), p. 349.

30 Famous above all for his leading role in Luis Buñuel's *L'Âge d'or* (1930), Modot had already performed for Renoir in *La Vie est à nous* (1936) *La Grande Illusion* and *La Marseillaise*, and would reappear in *French Cancan* (1954).

31 Lee Russell [Peter Wollen], 'Jean Renoir', *New Left Review*, May/June 1964, p. 59.

32 See Narboni (ed.), *Jean Renoir*, p. 292.

33 Dalio, *Mes années folles*, p. 127.

34 This is the name of the emphatically Jewish character that Dalio played in Renoir's *La Grande Illusion*.

35 Attributed to the notorious Bardèche and Brasillach in Dalio, *Mes années folles*, p. 132.

36 Ibid., p. 131.

37 A technician is visible in the mirror as Nora Gregor sits down, and even more so as he moves out of view.

38 Some readings of the movie want to escape this uncertainty. Olivier Curchod's fine edition of the screenplay asserts that Christine is planning revenge on Robert. That would typecast her too much as an affronted wife in the theatrical and operatic tradition (Curchod, *La Regle du jeu*, p. 166).

39 Lorraine LoBianco and David Thompson (eds), *Jean Renoir: Correspondance 1913–1978* (France: Plon, 1998), p. 286.

40 Letter from Renoir to Thomas Bishop, 7 May 1956, quoted in Thomas Bishop, *Pirandello and the French Theater* (New York: New York University Press, 1960), p. 143.

41 Renoir, *My Life*, p. 136.

42 Ibid., pp. 69–71.

43 Ibid., p. 172.

44 On disc 2, Criterion Collection DVD.

45 Paulette Dubost, *C'est court, la vie* (Paris: Flammarion, 1992), p. 98.

46 Interview in *Pour Vous*, 28 June 1939.

47 Interview in *Image et Son*, No. 282, March 1974, quoted in Christopher Faulkner, *The Social Cinema of Jean Renoir* (Princeton, NJ: Princeton University Press, 1986), p. 141.

48 One remarkable instance of the frame crowded in depth: as Schumacher barges towards the ballroom, gun in hand, pursuing Marceau among the dancing guests, the far background of the image framed by the open doorway offers the figures of Jurieu and La Chesnaye hauling the vigorously resistant body of Geneviève upstairs. Their figures would scarcely be identifiable if we had not seen the start of this action some seconds ago (see image at bottom of p. 93).

49 Narboni (ed.), *Jean Renoir*, p. 298.

Credits

La Règle du jeu
France/1939

'Fantasia dramatique de'
Jean Renoir
Scenario and Dialogue
Jean Renoir
Director of Photography
[Jean] Bachelet
Art Director
[Eugène] Lourié
Editors
Marguerite [Houllé-Renoir]
Mme [Marthe] Huguet
Music [Extracts by]
[Wolfgang Amadeus] Mozart
[Pierre-Alexandre] Monsigny
Music [Arranged and Conducted by]
Roger Desormières
[Desormière]

[Scenario and Dialogue] Collaborator
[Carl] Koch
Production Manager
Claude Renoir
Unit Manager
[Raymond] Pillion
[aka Pillon]
Administration
Camille François
[Assistant] Art Director
[Max] Douy

Assistant [Directors]
André Zwobada
Henri Cartier [-Bresson]
[Assistant] Photography
Jacques Lemare
[Camera Operator]
[Jean-Paul] Alphen
[Camera Assistant]
Alain Renoir
[Camera Assistant]
Still Photography
Sam Lévin
Dresses by
La Maison Chanel
Sound Engineer
De Bretagne
[Joseph de Bretagne]
Sound Recorded on
Western Electric
supplied by Paris-Studios-Cinéma
(Billancourt)
Prints
G. M. Film
Opticals
Kinoptik

Uncredited
Production Company
NEF – Nouvelle Édition Française
Producer
Jean Renoir
Production Secretary
Yvonne Bénézech
Assistant Director
Carl Koch

Continuity
Dido Freire
Make-up
Paul Ralph
Hair
Suzy Berton
Property Master
Laure Lourié
Properties
Christofle
Additional Music Extracts by
Frédéric Chopin
Gaston Claret
Camille François
Earl Rose
Camille Saint-Saëns
Louis Desormes
Lucien Delonnel
Léon Garnier
Eugene Rosi
Francis Salabert
Johann Strauss
Vincent Scotto
Music Arranger
Joseph Kosma
Hunt Scene Consultant
Antoine 'Tony' Corteggiani
Publicity
Georges Cravenne

CAST
Nora Grégor
Marquise Christine de La Cheyniest
Paulette Dubost
Lisette Schumacher, her maid

Mila Parély
Geneviève de Marras
Odette Talazac
Madame Charlotte de
La Plante
Claire Gérard
Madame de La Bruyère
Anne Mayen
Jackie, Christine's niece
Lise Élina
radio reporter at
Le Bourget
[Marcel] Dalio
Marquis Robert de
La Cheyniest
[Julien] Carette
Marceau, poacher
Roland Toutain
André Jurieux
Gaston Modot
Édouard Schumacher,
gamekeeper
Jean Renoir
Octave
Pierre Magnier
the general
Eddy Debray
Corneille, butler
Pierre Nay
Monsieur de St Aubin
[Richard] Francœur
Monsieur de La Bruyère
Léon Larive
Jean, cook

NB: Most printed and
online sources suggest
that the character name
Cheyniest should be
spelled Chesnaye and
that Marras should be
Marrast. The information
presented above is
transcribed from the
'restored version'
on-screen credits.

Uncredited
**Antoine 'Tony'
Corteggiani**
Berthelin, huntsman
Nicolas Amato
Cava, South
American guest
Georges Forster
Dick, gay friend
of Geneviève
André Zwobada
engineer at airplane
company Caudron
Henri Cartier-Bresson
William, English servant
Jacques Beauvais
Adolphe
Bob Mathieu
Robert's driver
Marcel Melrac
Christine's driver
Gitta Hardy
Mitzi
Maurice Marceau
first watchman
Celestin
kitchen boy

Jenny Hélia
Germaine, waitress
Camille François
voice on radio
Ernest Pointard
Pointard
Père Tabourel
gardener
Jean Nérys
Jurieux's mechanic
Maurice Sarlande
servant/guest
Charles Lamy
bearded huntsman
Jeanne de Carol
Jacques Goujon
Madame Guérassy
Olga Modot
Marguerite de Morlaye
guests at La Colinière

Production Details
Filmed from 22 February
to 19 May 1939.
Additional filming on
30 May, with final
shooting taking place as
late as mid-June 1939.
Filmed on location in
Paris and Sologne (Loiret,
Loir-et-Cher and Cher),
France, and at Studios
Pathé-Cinéma (Joinville-
le-Pont, Val-de-Marne,
France). 35mm.
Black and white. 1.37:1.
Mono sound –
Western Electric.

Release Details

French theatrical release by Gaumont (general release on 8 July 1939; Paris premiere: 7 July 1939). Running time: 91 minutes (cut to c. 84 minutes).

French theatrical re-release by DPF – Distribution Parisienne de Films (released in 1945). Running time: 85 minutes.

UK theatrical release by New London Film Society c. late 1946, BBFC certificate A (passed with no cuts). Registered at 7,601 feet (84 minutes 27 seconds).

US theatrical release (as 'The Rules of the Game') by Cine Classics (released on 8 April 1950). Running time: 85 minutes.

French theatrical re-release ('restored version') by Les Grands Films Classiques (shown at the 1959 Venice Film Festival, general release on 23 April 1965). Running time: 106 minutes. 'Restored version' title card reads: 'Jean Gaborit and Jacques Durand have restored this film to its original form with the approval and advice of Jean Renoir who dedicates this revival to the memory of Andre Bazin.'

Credits compiled by Julian Grainger

Select Bibliography

Some key books, mainly in English, not cited in the Notes.

Bertin, Célia, *Jean Renoir: A Life in Pictures*, trans. M. and L. Muellner (Baltimore, MD: Johns Hopkins University Press, 1991).

Bert Cardullo (ed.), *Jean Renoir Interviews* (Jackson: University Press of Mississippi, 2005).

Olivier Curchod and Christopher Faulkner, *La Règle du jeu: scénario original de Jean Renoir* (Paris: Nathan, 1999).

Raymond Durgnat, *Jean Renoir* (London: Studio Vista, 1975).

Peter Harcourt, *Six European Directors* (London: Penguin, 1974).

Martin O'Shaughnessy, *Jean Renoir* (Manchester: Manchester University Press, 2000).

Gilberto Perez, *The Material Ghost – Films and Their Medium* (Baltimore, MD: Johns Hopkins University Press, 1998).

William Rothman, *The 'I' of the Camera* (New York: Cambridge University Press, 2004).

François Truffaut (ed.), *Jean Renoir by André Bazin*, trans. W. W. Halsey and William H. Simon (New York: Simon & Schuster, 1973).

George M. Wilson, *Narration in Light* (Baltimore, MD: Johns Hopkins University Press, 1986).